Virtual Organizations and Beyond

Wiley Series in Practical Strategy

Published titles

Business Unit Strategy
Segev

Forthcoming titles

The Turbulence Concept: Strategic Management for
Difficult Times
Ansoff

Strategic Market Planning: A Blueprint for Success
McNamee

Virtual Organizations and Beyond

Discover Imaginary Systems

Bo Hedberg, Göran Dahlgren, Jörgen Hansson
and Nils-Göran Olve

JOHN WILEY & SONS
Chichester • New York • Weinheim • Brisbane • Singapore • Toronto

Other Wiley Editorial Offices

John Wiley & Sons, Inc., 605 Third Avenue,
New York, NY 10158-0012, USA

WILEY-VCH Verlag GmbH, Pappelallee 3,
D-69469 Weinheim, Germany

Jacaranda Wiley Ltd, 33 Park Road, Milton,
Queensland 4064, Australia

John Wiley & Sons (Asia) Pte Ltd, 2 Clementi Loop #02-01,
Jin Xing Distripark, Singapore 129809

John Wiley & Sons (Canada) Ltd, 22 Worcester Road,
Rexdale, Ontario M9W 1L1, Canada

Library of Congress Cataloging-in-Publication Data

Imaginära organisationer.   English
    Virtual organizations and beyond / Bo Hedberg . . . [et al.].
       p. cm.—Wiley series in practical strategy)
    Includes bibliographical references and index.
    ISBN 0-471-97493-5 (alk. paper)
    1. Virtual reality in management. 2. Organization.
    3. Information society. I. Hedberg, Bo, 1944- . II. Title.
    III. Series.
    HD30.2122.14513 1997
    302.3´5—dc21   97-8658
                                         CIP

British Library Cataloguing in Publication Data

A catalogue record for this book is available from the British Library

ISBN 0-471-97493-5

Typeset in 11/13pt Times by Laser Words, Madras, India
Printed and bound in Great Britain by Biddles Ltd, Guildford and King's Lynn.
This book is printed on acid-free paper responsibly manufactured from sustainable forestation,
for which as least two trees are planted for each one used for paper production.

Contents

Series Foreword

The aim of this series is to provide managers with books on strategy, strategic management, and strategic change, which are helpful, practical, and provide guidance for the practical application of sound concepts in real situations.

In the mid-1960s when the subject of planning began to emerge, the whole literature could have been listed on one or two sheets of paper. It was easy to decide which books to read, because so few were available. This state of affairs changed rapidly, and the scope of the subject has moved from a focus on formal planning to a broader view which merges with the literature of leadership, change management, strategic analysis and organization. Modern writing sees the organization and its strategies in an integrated way, and there are many, often conflicting, theories about the "right" way to formulate strategies and practice strategic management.

Management does not take an academic interest in theories, but is concerned about what works best in the situation in which it operates. Hence this series. Each book is conceptually sound, and gives proper acknowledgement to the originators of concepts and ideas, but the emphasis is on using the concepts or methods, rather than academic argument.

Business school faculty and students are also concerned with the application of theories and will find much in these books to supplement the more academic texts.

In this series the aim is to give the reader clear guidance on how to make the subject of the book work in his or her own situation, while at the same time taking care to ensure that the books do not over-simplify situations. Check lists and questionnaires are included when they aid the aims of the book, and examples are given. The experience of the author in actually applying the concepts, rather than just knowing about them, is intended to show through the writing.

The series will make complex matters understandable. We hope that it will become a catalyst that helps managers make a difference to the strategic performance of their organizations.

David Hussey
David Hussey & Associates
Editor of Journal of Strategic Change

Preface

This book is the combined result of our research and training as researchers and our interaction with business as consultants and corporate advisors. Our ambition is to combine these two worlds; the one of studying and revealing new patterns of business through scientific research and the one of organizing, strategizing, and structuring business through management. We attempt to tie these two worlds together through some conceptual models and also through a number of short case studies which are based on our ongoing research.

This is a book about the "virtual enterprise" or, as we prefer to say, "imaginary organizations". We want the reader to discover imaginary organizations (IO) *as a powerful perspective on business*. Many *new* enterprises could easily be described and analyzed as imaginary organizations. They were built that way from the very start. But imaginary organizations are also embedded in many *old and mature* enterprises. Or better, many existing companies could efficiently be restructured or combined with partners through IO arrangements. The IO perspective then serves as a blueprint for business development and renewal.

The research program on Imaginary Organizations began at the School of Business at Stockholm University in 1992 and is foreseen to continue at least until the turn of the century. When the program began, we were not aware of the term "virtual organizations" that later appeared in the international management literature.

But we were aware of the fact that a growing number of organizations, in business and in public administration, began to escape the language of accounting, the practice of management, and the laws and regulations that were set up to guide business, labor relations, and investment management. In short, business was about to leave the field of business administration behind.

As teachers in business schools we were disturbed by the fact that textbooks and curricula by and large neglected these emerging new realities. As researchers we saw numerous interesting challenges. The perspective of imaginary organizations turned many established knowledge areas upside down. Imaginary organizations existed far outside their "boundaries". Leaders were expected to lead and inspire people whom they did not employ. The real assets of these companies were not accounted for, and what was accounted for was not always very important.

Anyone who was able to see this in the IO perspective would share our excitement about the business opportunities which are opening up and possibly also our concern about the need to develop our language on organizations and management so as to identify and account for these new aspects of organizing for modern business.

This book is primarily written for people who are interested in business development and business renewal in the age of the information society. Particularly we want to reach those who find it difficult to see development opportunities in current organizations. We are also eager to strengthen those entrepreneurs who are about to start new enterprises and who possess good ideas and a lot of motivation, but who lack capital or other necessary support structures. We want to show them blueprints from which colleagues in other industries and in other parts of the world have built rapidly growing businesses using others' manpower, others' capital, and others' production facilities. There are ways to grow without becoming bigger. Of course, we also want to address bankers and investors so that they see and understand these new patterns of growing business and dare to venture capital therein.

We wrote this book in Swedish two years ago. It sold very well and opened up a world of contacts with industry and public administration. We also discovered that the book was useful in teaching organization design, strategy, and organization behavior in business schools, although the book is primarily written as a management book.

This book is the result of team work, first, within the group of authors and then within the OD Group at CEPRO Management Consultants, in Stockholm, our joint practice and endeavor. We also owe many thanks to our client companies. Bo Hedberg has worked closely with academic colleagues and doctoral students within the research program at the School of Business. Benevolent research funding for this program has been given by the HSFR (the Swedish Foundation for Research in Social Sciences and the Humanities), NUTEK (the Swedish National Board for Industrial and Technical Development), and KFB (the Swedish Transport Communications Research Board).

Gunilla Gustafsson coordinated the book project, first in Swedish and then for an extended, international version of the original book. To her, to our CEPRO colleagues and clients, and to our fellow researchers and, of course, to our publisher, many thanks.

Bo Hedberg, Göran Dahlgren, Jörgen Hansson, Nils-Göran Olve,
Stockholm, 1997

CEPRO Management Consultants,
Box 440, S-101 28 Stockholm, Sweden
Telephone: +46 (0) 84029800
Fax: +46 (0) 8105469
E-mail: Company@cepro.se
Homepage: www.cepro.se

1

The Imaginary Organization— Discover a New Perspective

INTRODUCTION

What we see tells us where we are and what to do. We chose the illustration on the back cover to symbolize our principal message. This work of art, prepared by computer and entitled *Two Hands,* appears at first glance to represent a rather intricate pattern of blue, white, and red, repeated in something resembling rows. The superficial pattern may retain the viewer's interest for a short while, but it hardly gives an impression of being a work of art. If there were nothing more to it, *Two Hands* would not merit further thought.

But there is more. If you concentrate on the center of the picture and try to focus in depth, you will find after a while that the image changes. Suddenly the superficial pattern disappears and you see what the picture actually represents: two hands reaching towards you. The picture has become three-dimensional. Your eyes relax, and you restfully contemplate it in depth. Now it is all so simple and obvious. And if you have experienced this transformation once, it is easier the next time you look at the picture. We can train our eyes and our imagination to see what lies beneath the surface.

The purpose of this book is to present a new a way of looking at organizations, a new perspective. We call it the perspective of 'the imaginary organization'. The organizations/companies presented both exist and do not exist. On the surface there are a number of units which function together in some way. Only when the viewer focuses on the in-depth dimension does the exciting transformation occur. The pieces of the puzzle fit together to form a clear, obvious and cohesive new organization: an imaginary organization.

This book is thus partly about the new companies which are often referred to as virtual companies. But mostly it is about a new way to look at old companies and make them grow, and to create new companies which transcend conventional boundaries. The book is intended to develop a perspective that will enhance the reader's ability to understand companies and to develop them further. The latter task becomes easier when you focus on the true image, as is the case with the cover illustration of the book. When the conventional structure fades out and the in-depth structure emerges, existing boundaries disappear and new relationships become obvious. There is no mystery to it, no hocus-pocus. Just a new and powerful way to view reality and to interpret it. It is a matter of reframing (Watzlawick et al, 1974).

Let us begin with examples of some companies.

Skandia AFS

Skandia AFS (Assurance and Financial Services) is a group of companies within the leading Swedish insurance company, Skandia AB. While the parent is a fairly conventional service enterprise, AFS is a highly successful, fast-growing, and very interesting imaginary organization.

Skandia AFS prospers from the growing concern of people in many countries that retirement systems and other welfare arrangements are endangered and may not deliver on their promises. Therefore, families and individuals are increasing their savings. Skandia is able to collect a portion of these savings and places them with fund managers who promise to beat inflation. Skandia AFS is a global savings organization with unit-link arrangements to tie those savings to growth investments.

In 1996 Skandia AFS operates in 14 countries on four continents outside Scandinavia. Some 60-odd people make up the headquarters, and they are mainly located in Sweden and in Shelton, CT, USA. An additional 2200 Skandia employees run the national companies.

But, these people engage some 70,000 partners in various countries in the enterprise. The partners are mostly money managers or financial consultants. In Spain a major savings bank collects household savings for placement through Skandia. The outer circle consists of around 1,200,000 customers, or "contracts" as described in Skandia's *Supplement* to the *1996 Annual Report* to the shareholders (Figure 1.1).

The leadership of Skandia AFS often uses the term "*federation*" to describe the way the business is organized. The company operates in between a global market for savings and a global market for investments. The core company acts as an exchange system between these two markets. Partners interact directly with clients (households) and investment opportunities. AFS, like the Skandia group in general, is of course a publicly quoted company with shareholders, boards of directors, and directives from the top executives and downwards. Thus, the financial capital works through a hierarchy; and so does the structural capital—the knowledge, procedures, and manuals

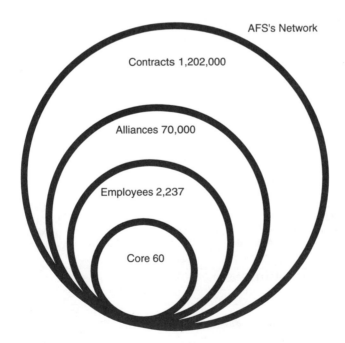

Figure 1.1 Skandia AFS as an imaginary organization (Skandia Annual Report 1996: Supplement)

which AFS has managed to formalize and store in its structure and processes. However, the market capital (customers and local networks) and the knowledge capital possessed by money managers and fund specialists in the partner network, work from the market and upwards in the hierarchy. In the latter sense, one could claim that Skandia AFS is a federative organization in which the power and dynamics come from the markets and are delegated upwards according to the principle of subsidiarity (Figure 1.2).

With around 2300 on the payroll, another 70,000 partners, and more than 1,200,000 customers, CEO Jan Carendi says that in order to lead the company he has to realize that he is managing a "voluntary organization". If these people around the world do not give their best by their own free will, he has no power to command them. In order to keep the AFS network together, he attempts to create a challenging vision, fast feedback on performance, and a "high-trust culture". Everyone in this voluntary organization has to be a "trustee" who deserves the trust of others and who trusts his/her collaborators.

Another way to "glue" the organization together has been to provide money managers and representatives on the market with excellent IT support. Thus, 18,000 CD-ROM copies of a system called ASSESS were distributed in the USA before Christmas 1995.

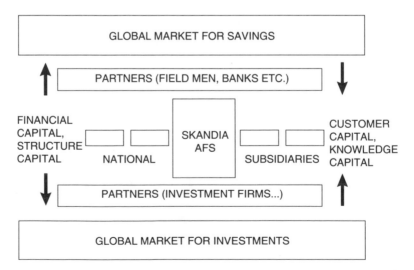

Figure 1.2 Skandia AFS, a combination of federation and hierarchy

The ASSESS system contains a multimedia presentation of American Skandia (the US branch of AFS), but its real value lies in the sales-support system. AFS experts and other national expertise help the salesman to explain various savings programs and tax consequences to the client. Also, the fund managers appear on the laptop screen to describe their business, their track record, and their investment policies. The ASSESS system does an excellent job in helping the salesmen to make the financial products understandable and to make the investment experts human and trustworthy. A new release of ASSESS with more storage capacity on CD-ROM will also contain a "virtual university", with short courses for the continuing education that financial advisers are required to take, pass, and have recorded in order to remain authorized.

A global management information system is another way to keep the world-wide organization together. The IT infrastructure also allows existing national companies to provide, e.g. back-office support for newly established subsidiaries. Thus, the back-office work for the pioneer company in Mexico and in Japan is managed from Shelton, Conn. Connecticut. In general, when new national companies are formed, AFS subsidiaries in other countries, together with headquarters, provide the financial products, the organization, market communication systems, and administrative programs. As a consequence of its ability to move rapidly and to be very flexible, Skandia AFS has been the first company to establish itself on national markets in many countries following deregulation. AFS's rhetoric uses the term "process edge" and pictures AFS as a mediator (product development, packaging, and administration) between fund management and distribution which is handled by partners (Figure 1.3).

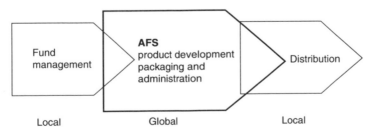

Figure 1.3 Skandia AFS's process focus

Multi-dimensional reporting, as expressed in Balanced Score Cards—which account for intellectual capital—and in the special Skandia version called "The Navigator", have been used to enrich and develop the feedback and reporting systems (see also Figure 2.2 in Chapter 2).

GANT

In only a few years GANT gained an interesting position on the market for Swedish ready-to-wear men's clothing. From this Swedish base GANT is now growing from country to country in Europe. Few men of lower to upper middle age can have missed the appeal of GANT's advertisements or catalogs. GANT brings what looks like American college and East Coast fashion to Europe and makes it available to male consumers with money to spend and a certain feeling for quality.

Many Swedes see GANT as an American manufacturer of ready-to-wear clothing. The two seasonal catalogs bring to mind America's East Coast. You see handsome men with pomaded or tousled hair and dazzling smiles, dressed in casual and rather colorful rugby jerseys, yachtsmen's pants, and windbreakers.

It is true that the GANT clothing factory and trademark originated in the USA; careful search will sometimes turn up GANT articles from the old American days. And the USA was where the owners of Pyramid Sportswear, the driving force behind the idea known as GANT, bought the license and the rights to the brand name. But the GANT articles which we Europeans know and wear do not come from American clothing factories, but from an imaginary organization based in Sweden. The center of operations is a Swedish company, Pyramid Sportswear AB. The brand name, collections, production, and retailer network are all the work of Pyramid. Pyramid Sportswear finds designers, identifies trends, contracts out quality-assured production, and cultivates a retailer network using catalogs, advertising, image-creating activities, and sales support in the form of a customer data base, active inventory and tracking systems, etc. (Figure 1.4).

A systematically designed customer data base, and extremely detailed and up-to-date reporting of shipments and current sales,

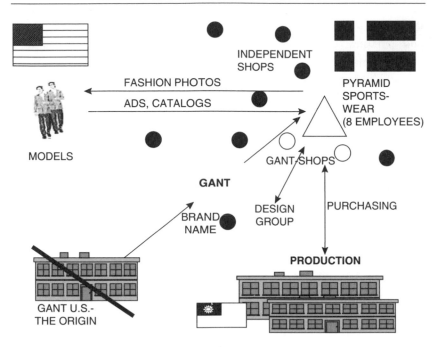

Figure 1.4 An imaginary perspective on the GANT organization

are two central elements which enable the imaginary GANT organization to exist and thrive. Remote quality control in interaction with temporary partners is another ingredient. Without modern information technology this supporting structure could not work.

GANT may be regarded as a rather clear-cut illustration of how one or more persons with a business concept but with limited resources—or at least a desire to limit the resources committed and to concentrate on essentials—can build an enterprise around an idea. The brand name, fashion creators, models, catalogs, stores, factories, customer lists, and inventory systems are co-ordinated into what appears to the customer as the successful GANT company. But behind the scene is Pyramid Sportswear, a number of selected men's clothing stores, freelance photographers, designers, catalog producers, and ready-made-clothing factories, the services of which are procured and quality-controlled from time to time. The whole is considerably larger than the sum of its parts. The partner enterprises and the individual actors in the GANT network are linked together in a variety of ways, from commercial contracts to personal contacts and personal chemistry. GANT is in no way unique in the new clothing industry. The new textile industrialists are "tailors without thread". Other Swedish examples are Peak Performance, Boomerang, and Jockey. Benetton in Italy, BOSS in Germany, and Bogner in Austria are others.

Organizations like these, as we perceive and describe them, have existed for quite some time. They need not be especially sophisticated. And they can sometimes function without computers and telecommunications. As a matter of fact, the garment industry is somehow returning to patterns which existed during a pre-industrial era where patrons traveled with horse and carriage to connect production, which took place in farms and cottages in the countryside. And the "virtual university" existed long before connections were measured in bytes per second. An example of this is Liber–Hermods.

Liber–Hermods

Since the turn of the century, 4 million Swedes have studied at the Hermods Correspondence Institute. In 1965, when the institute was doing best, the correspondence courses were arranged so that 25–30 regular employees could engage 400 "temporary" teachers throughout the country to correct examinations, etc. Thereafter, the Hermods concept of business lost ground as new kinds of schools were established; strictly speaking, only one upper secondary correspondence school remained of the previous 14. But the institute still had its reputation and the loyalty of customers and former temporary teachers.

The Liber publishing group bought Hermods in 1975, primarily for the latter's publishing operations. The new owners seemed to find Hermods a little outdated and tried to give the name a low profile. Hermods still fulfilled the important function of providing education to the children of expatriate Swedes serving in the diplomatic corps, companies operating abroad, and the missionary societies. But the home market was declining.

For several years in the 1980s, Hermods was involved in a highly publicized co-operative arrangement which included educational radio and TV and a number of colleges and universities. Courses in data processing, history of art, languages, and environmental science were provided through TV programs, books, and Hermods' traditional assignment correction and course administration. The arrangement may have been an initial attempt at creating a Swedish Open University; it was definitely an imaginary educational organization.

By the 1990s times had changed again. Both at the Swedish Department of Education and in local government, people have become much more open-minded about how schools should be organized. Business has realized the need for life-long learning. New ways have been found to exploit the competence which Hermods had acquired and retained. We are no longer talking about purely long-distance education, but about combining materials for individual study with courses led by an instructor. The combinations are put together by Hermods, which guarantees quality and engages the necessary partners. For example, local school districts which otherwise would have to send pupils to a neighbouring district may make an arrangement with Hermods. The local school provides teachers and classrooms, arranges the schedule, etc., while Hermods supplies the materials, contributes to the continuing education of the teachers, and administers the examinations. Prior to an examination, students can attend preparatory courses at a more limited number of other locations in the country. Under this arrangement the local upper secondary school can continue to function when it would otherwise have to be closed for lack of pupils. The Hermods profile is intended to be low but identifiable; the support provided should be appreciated locally as an asset and a guarantee of quality, but the school should be regarded as the local one.

There are similar solutions for companies which would like to have their "own" programs for employees but cannot provide the necessary competence on their own, and for the schooling of expatriate Swedes. Hermods is presently in the process of accreditation to administer examinations for college courses. Modern IT may soon lead to further changes in the mix of individual study/teacher-controlled instruction/long-distance education.

In the 1980s Hermods cut its operations in half. Much of the essential know-how was possessed by the temporaries rather than the limited number of regular employees. But the loyalty of the former temporaries was so strong that when growth recently returned, it was possible to recreate the network of necessary competence: "All they had to do was mention Hermods and people turned up".

The Hermods Correspondence Institute was based on systems of communication, though not at all on modern information technology. The founder, the IO-leader, had a concept of a nation-wide market (all children, primarily in rural areas, who were willing and intellectually able to study, but who had been prevented from doing so by living conditions, by having to work, or by geographic remoteness). He also had a concept of distribution—communication by mail. He then staffed the organization with teachers working on the side, gradually adding authors of educational materials, an organization to correct examinations, etc. From the very beginning Hermods was a network in which operations to a large extent were conducted outside the enterprise proper. This arrangement was modified a number of times as the years passed. Hermods has made use of local school and college facilities, individual teachers, radio and TV producers, etc., as well as colleges and educational associations. The Hermods concept may sometimes seem outmoded and on the decline, but in fact it is very much alive today.

To capture the invisible—the power of imagination

Imaginary ... From landscape to mindscape. From work place to work space. Out of sight, but not out of mind.

Imagine ... Use your fantasy ... use your senses ... make sense ... and see reality in a new perspective.

Reframe reality ... Therapists successfully use reframing (Watzlawick et al, 1974) as a method of treatment for groups and individuals. If clients can reformulate their problems, solutions are often readily available.

The British–Canadian researcher Gareth Morgan (1993) identified five principal functions of our *imagination*:

- Improving our ability to see and understand situations in new ways.
- Finding images for new ways of organizing.
- Creating a shared understanding.
- Personal empowerment.
- Developing the capacity for continuous self-organization.

In this book we want to present a new frame of reference and to illustrate our reasoning and observations with cases taken from our consulting experience and research efforts, so that the reader will see what we see: new patterns for doing business which already exist and which are being developed further. The clearest examples are those of the new and somewhat spectacular companies, often outside of traditional industries. But the IO (imaginary organization) perspective may be used in the latter area as well; once we have opened our eyes to the imaginary organization, we also find it present to a significant degree in mature companies, which we might consider rather conventional.

Even in the 1950s, executives and researchers were talking about externalities, invisible items in the balance sheet. "Cultivated markets", "image", and "know-how" had value but were not readily recognized under generally accepted accounting principles. Consequently, obvious investments were treated as expenses, and significant assets and liabilities were not shown in balance sheets.

The 1960s and 1970s marked a growing interest in Human Resource Accounting. Starting in the USA, ambitious attempts were later made to treat employees as a resource and to determine the accounting consequences of various actions taken in the personnel area (Flamholtz, 1985; Johansson & Nilsson, 1992). The latter approach was successfully adopted in the first academic and practical works on the Social Audit.

The notion of the *knowledge-intensive firm* also recognized that major assets of modern companies can be difficult enough to describe and often impossible to reflect in the accounting system. Developments in *Service Management* (Normann, 1984) and in *Relationship Marketing* (Gummesson, 1995, 1996) brought up customer relations, customer data bases, delivery systems, and value constellations as other important elements of successful business. Again, these new components and resources were obviously not included in the language of accounting, organization charts and the focus of traditional management (Figure 1.5.).

The recurring theme in all these attempts and approaches is to make visible what is invisible. Together we have gradually discovered that managerial economics fails to cover important aspects of doing business. There are significant invisible assets, invisible links, and operations which transcend conventional boundaries. If you can

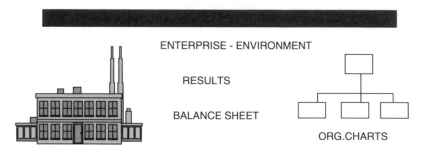

COMPETENCE NETWORKS RELATIONS
CUSTOMER BASE VALUE-CREATION
REPUTATION STRATEGIC ALLIANCES
BUSINESS IDEA

ENTERPRISE - ENVIRONMENT

RESULTS

BALANCE SHEET

ORG.CHARTS

Figure 1.5 The visible and invisible worlds of business

see the invisible and make it work for you, you can find interesting ways to develop your company. It is symptomatic that books entitled *Invisibly Occupied* (Arbnor et al, 1980) and *The Invisible Balance Sheet* (Sveiby et al, 1986) (English translations of Swedish titles) have been published. It appears that the invisible elements of business are worth developing.

In the USA the phenomenon to which we are referring is called "virtual organizations". By the early 1980s there were already computers with so called virtual memories, memories with "overflow capacity" and thus capable of functioning for practical purposes as if they were larger than they really were. At a time when we are becoming fascinated by the virtual reality of the computer age, the possibility of using information technology to move around and experience sensations in a virtually created world, we find in the popular American business press an ever-growing number of virtual companies which extend beyond the confines of traditional business organizations.

Whether one uses the term "virtual" or "imaginary" is really a matter of taste. The *Concise Oxford Dictionary* defines "virtual" as "not physically existing as such but made by software to do so". This definition goes well with virtual memories and virtual realities, but also, mostly, with the virtual enterprise. Also the "imaginary" is something that exists in our minds rather than in the physical world. Martin (1996) refers to degrees of "virtualness" in business firms, and we find the perspective of imaginary organizations useful in enterprises which are less or more imaginary. While "virtual", to our taste, takes us to the world of technologies, "imaginary" carries more flavors from the world of humanities. Thus, the authors of this book have chosen to use the collective concepts of imaginary systems and the imaginary organization. The reader who prefers the perhaps more fashionable concept of the virtual enterprise can easily substitute imaginary for virtual.

We developed our language around this phenomenon some years ago and before we were really aware that the phrase "virtual" would dominate the scene (Welles, 1983; Davidson & Malone, 1992). "Imaginary organizations" is also the name of a research project which has been conducted for a number of years at the School of Business of Stockholm University. The project is under the direction of Bo Hedberg, one of the authors of this book. Like the other authors, Bo Hedberg is also a management consultant at CEPRO, where we have found in recent years that the IO perspective is a very powerful aid to understanding and developing the businesses of companies.

We are writing this book to pass this business-oriented perspective on to senior company executives, as well as to other managers responsible for profitability and development in companies and other organizations. Our objective is to establish a new perspective on business and to illustrate new opportunities for developing new enterprises and for renewed development in existing ones.

First, a brief frame of reference.

A FRAME OF REFERENCE—DEFINITIONS AND KEY CONCEPTS

We use the term "the imaginary organization" to indicate a particular perspective on companies and other organizations. Let us begin with a definition—We may say that:

> The perspective of the imaginary organization refers to a system in which assets, processes, and actors critical to the "focal" enterprise exist and function both inside and outside the limits of the enterprise's conventional "landscape" formed by its legal structure, its accounting, its organigrams, and the language otherwise used to describe the enterprise.

The imaginary organization is thus a perspective revealing new enterprises which can utilize imagination, information technology, alliances, and other networks to organize and sustain a boundary-transcending activity; here the relevant organization is predominantly imaginary.

The imaginary organization is also useful as a perspective on existing enterprises in that it can facilitate the discovery of significant resources and possible combinations which would promote efficiency, business development, and the regeneration of the enterprise.

But the imaginary organization (IO) cannot be perceived by everyone. Like the theme of the cover illustration of this book, an imaginary vision requires a focus and an act of will. The viewer becomes absorbed in the painting. The leader of the enterprise is looking for an overall picture. With practice the act of will becomes easier. When the picture is evoked, certain things become evident. A new equilibrium is established.

Imaginary organizations are artificial representations of what we see. They are conceived and directed by one or more actors using an IO perspective. Here we find no generally accepted terminology. We considered the terms "IO-leader" and "IO architect", and used the term "Imaginator" (*imaginatör*) in the Swedish original publication. However, the words "IO-leader" and "imaginator" are used interchangeably in this English text. We are convinced that business leaders who design new imaginary organizations do so consciously and with a fairly explicit vision of the final result in mind. However, it does not follow that they are capable of putting their vision into words or describing it to others. But they do see the depth dimension of the "painting", and they act accordingly.

The same reasoning applies to the renovation of existing companies. Imagination and vision are required to identify the core competence as a platform for further advancement and to find the simplifications and new combinations which can permit the company to develop. As in the building industry, the resulting change may involve renovation, reconstruction, or extension. The IO-leader sees the imaginary potential of the existing company and builds further on that basis.

As noted above, the imaginary organization is also a perspective which—when applied to existing enterprises—reveals the imaginary logic and resources inherent in established operations and facilitates and supports efforts to build and develop new systems from this base. Information technology, networks and alliances, attraction, and customer relationships are examples of important resources for conducting and co-ordinating operations (imaginary systems) which extend beyond the limits of the organization and which are based on co-operation and synergy with external actors.

Awareness of the possibilities offered by the IO can help the entrepreneur to develop a company even when conventional resources, particularly capital, are very limited. The IO perspective can provide a model for expansion without growth, for linking synergy to energy, and for involving many more people than just the employees in the service of the company's concept of business.

Let us now begin by summarizing our frame of reference and the key concepts which we will later use in our descriptions and analyses.

The *IO-leader* can be male or female, an individual or a small group, with a *will* to accomplish something. Consciously or intuitively, the IO-leader creates a *strategic map* showing how a new business arrangement will be put together in an imaginary organization. The IO-leader also has a conception of the *core competence* of his own unit. This competence is later supplemented by the contributions of the partners and partner enterprises co-operating in the arrangement. The IO-leader's unit is called the *leader enterprise*. We thus have the picture shown in Figure 1.6 at the start. The next step is to define a *customer base*, one or more *delivery systems*, and the methods of *communication with customers* (Figure 1.7). When these steps have been completed, the IO-leader designs the production

INSIGHT ABOUT
CORE COMPETENCE

OPPORTUNITY   IO-   STRATEGIC
AND WILLINGNESS   LEADER   PLAN/
TO ACT   MENTAL MAP

LEADER
ENTERPRISE

Figure 1.6 The starting point

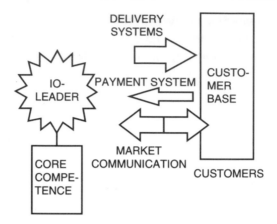

Figure 1.7   The market-oriented enterprise

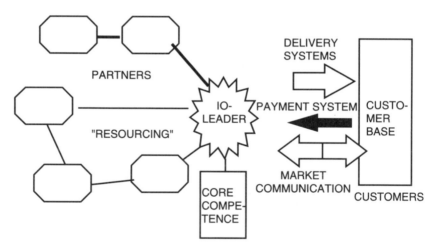

Figure 1.8   Resourcing the imaginary organization

system needed to produce the goods and/or services desired. The *leader enterprise*, the IO-leader's own company, performs an essential function here. One or more *partners* or *partner enterprises* are added to the network, which is managed and held together by the leader enterprise (Figure 1.8).

The employees of the leader enterprise will be referred to simply as *employees*. All persons (employees and others) working for the imaginary organization will be termed "*involvees*". The *I/E-ratio* is the ratio of involvees to employees; it indicates the leverage of the core competence created by the system.

Let us now try out our models and concepts in a little exercise in terminology involving *IKEA*, the well-known Swedish-based international furniture company.

IKEA

When the IO-leader, IKEA's Chairman Ingvar Kamprad, describes how he founded the company, he says, "I had this idea about distribution. Even as a boy I could see that there was a future in selling by mail-order. Distribution was too complicated at that time."

Thus, the company was founded on a concept of distribution. Selling furniture came along later. But early on, reaching out to the many "ordinary people" was a part of the IO-leader's strategic map. New elements were gradually added, like the "flat package" and "get the customer to help... pick-up directly from stock". The customer base was reinforced with the "Family concept", and certain kinds of customers were tied more closely to the company by the IKEA charge account. IKEA is the leader enterprise. The IO-leader, Ingvar Kamprad, had the will to create something important and to meet a customer need.

The core competence of the leader enterprise lies in its ability to combine modern design with easily transported furniture (flat packages), and then, through its catalog, mail-order system, and a growing number of stores, to function as intermediary between producer and customer. Ideally, the flat package and the interested customer arrive at the stock-room at the same time—in other words, just-in-time for each other.

For decades IKEA had no production facilities of its own and it still owns only a few small factories. With the market in mind, it turned to capable manufacturers, choosing those offering an optimal price/quality trade-off. IKEA works closely with its manufacturers in such areas as design, production methods, and quality assurance (ISO certification). The number of involvees in the entire IKEA operation has always greatly exceeded the number of IKEA employees.

It may be objected that IKEA in a number of ways is an ordinary company with various real assets in the form of buildings, offices, inventories, and equipment. That statement is clearly true. But what actually makes IKEA a unique and very valuable company is its concept of business—"The legacy of a furniture dealer", the IKEA culture, the basic "Family concept", and the network of contacts with furniture manufacturers in southern Sweden, in Eastern Europe, and elsewhere. In important ways, all of the actors involved here are pulling in the same direction, inspired by the ideas of Kamprad, the founder, and supported by the expertise of the IKEA headquarters staff. In the imaginary IKEA organization, the leader enterprise, IKEA, "owns" the customers. Partner enterprises are only admitted under the IKEA brand name and image. Customer communication, and learning from the market, are owned and controlled by IKEA.

Thus, the imaginary IKEA organization of today still embodies Kamprad's fundamental concepts. You will not find this imaginary organization in the accounting system or in the organization chart, but it is what makes IKEA great.

> Sometimes building a system from an IO perspective should have been a real alternative to the approach which was chosen and which led to what actually happened. Consider the case of SAS and the idea of "the Total Travel Experience" in another exercise of terminology.

SAS (Scandinavian Airlines System)

The IO-leader, Jan Carlzon, CEO of SAS in the period 1981–1993, and the SAS executive group around him, wanted to create more value for the customer by offering most of what is normally included in a business trip and which may cause the customer problems. Business travelers made up the customer base, hence SAS's claim to be "The Businessman's Airline".

RVC (the Royal Viking Card) and other devices were used to tie these customers more closely to the company. SAS arranged a value constellation around the transportation service itself. Financing (Diner's) and ground transportation (SAS Limousine), new hotel chains and a broad range of entertainment and leisure-time activities (SAS Leisure Group) were added.

Carlzon's successors then dismantled most of this bundle of services provided directly by SAS. As always when a strong leader has been replaced, it is difficult to make a balanced assessment of his strategy. From the perspective of "building an imaginary system around customer needs as perceived", the Total Travel Experience was a creative and interesting approach. What did not fit in, and what was probably the major mistake, was putting all these related services under SAS's own roof. Hotel management, personal financial services, and fleets of limousines have never been part of SAS's core competence. If instead SAS as the leader enterprise had consistently chosen to involve partner enterprises to beef up its range of customer services, while never owning and managing these operations extraneous to its system, the situation today might have looked a bit better.

What subsequently happened at SAS under the new CEO Jan Stenberg is interesting to analyze from an IO perspective. The initial steps taken should be viewed in light of an acute need to shore up the balance sheet and to start showing a profit as soon as possible. Selling the SAS Leisure Group (with its leading position in areas of strategic importance for customer contact) poses problems from an IO point of view. After all, isn't today's highly competitive airline industry suffering from a shortage of customers rather than airplanes? On the other hand, SAS's subsequent pattern of action, in allying itself with Lufthansa, Thai, and American Airlines, is consistent with an IO perspective. The Alcazar merger, which Jan Carlzon failed to push through, is now being recreated as a partnership system in which the competence and flight networks of several airlines are being joined together to serve a combined customer base. An integrated bonus system provides an incentive for customers to fly with the new alliance.

WHAT HOLDS THE IMAGINARY ORGANIZATION TOGETHER?

The imaginary organization (IO) is held together primarily by cohesive forces other than those used for conventional companies, such as capital, laws and contracts, customs, and tradition.

> *Trust* is probably the most important ingredient in the "organizational glue" that keeps an IO from coming apart. Some leaders in our studies even use the phrase "high-trust culture" to describe this glue.

Synergies constitute an important class of cohesive forces. Synergies may relate to the customer base, market communication, the delivery system, the production system, purchasing, or input goods.

We find another major category of cohesive forces in *information technology*. IT can make co-ordination possible over an area that otherwise would be too large from an economic or practical standpoint. It can reduce transaction costs to the point where a traditional hierarchy no longer serves a useful purpose. It can offer economies of scale in an efficacious infrastructure which no single company could set up. Examples might be a jointly owned computer network, mailing system, or other high-powered form of communication.

Various types of *contracts* providing mutual incentives constitute an additional form of cohesive force. *Royalty agreements* are the classic cement of publishing systems, but a whole variety of other binding forces are conceivable and in fact exist. However, many IOs are held together primarily by the unifying factor of a splendid *business concept*, or by the *vision* articulated by strong leadership. In practice, various combinations of these different kinds of cohesive forces are found in most organizations. A possible special case is the existence of a strong, threatening competitor which compels a number of otherwise independently-minded companies to join together in a more or less firm alliance.

VALUE CREATION

Systems may consist of several organizations working together to achieve economies of scale (or dominance) at a particular link in the succession of processes which add value along the line from producer to customer. Michael Porter of the Harvard Business School (Porter, 1985) termed this succession of links a *value chain*.

More commonly, however, systems for value creation take the form of a constellation, with the actual process of value creation in the center. A number of different goods and services create an attractive combination (an offer) for the customer. Rickard Normann calls this formation for value creation a *value constellation* (Normann & Ramirez, 1993) (Figure 1.9). In a value constellation different actors work together to create value for the customer.

Over time, systems can grow stronger and more robust, or weaker and more fragile. To some degree, they are always vulnerable.

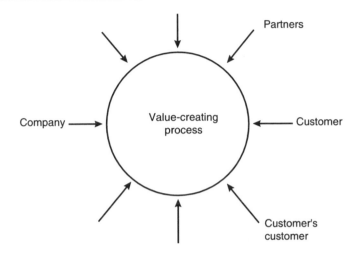

Figure 1.9 Creating a value constellation

Dominating the customer relationship, or "owning the customer", is important to keep from losing influence and the initiative in a value chain. Surely it also furnishes a position of strength for various forms of co-operative ventures that can coalesce along the chain.

In a robust system we find mutuality and symmetry in the relationships among the parties. It would seem quite possible to find ways to measure return on the investment in these relationships, just as conventional organizations naturally measure return on invested capital.

SUMMARY

We can identify three criteria to distinguish between the imaginary organization (IO) and "loosely coupled systems" (Weick, 1979) in general.

1. The IO consists of a number of components which are joined together in a pattern and in which the relationships among the components are based on purchasing/selling, a shared physical or information infrastructure, appeal of an idea, or, less often, a contract.

2. The IO has been purposefully designed by an IO-leader, who have built up the system from an original concept of the core competence and of the market.

3. Co-ordinating the core competence of the leader enterprise and that of each partner enterprise is critical to the competitiveness and survival of the IO.

In summary:

- The perspective of the "imaginary organization" helps us:
  — To make invisible resources visible.
  — To manage externalities.
  — To see what new structures are required.
  — To cultivate the core competence.
  — To develop the new cohesive forces.
  — To understand better the intuitive aspects of the business.

In the imaginary organization:

- The leader enterprise operates far outside its borders.
- Others' resources provide growth and flexibility.
- There are few employees, but many involvees.
- Clients are involved in value creation.
- Business culture encompasses the entire operation.
- Multiple accountings in multiple dimensions.
- *IT* is often an important facilitator.

Thus, the new enterprise is built by:

- Value creation for and with customers.
- A clear and attractive vision.
- Leadership and empowerment.
- Partnerships.
- Shared values.
- Imagination.
- Information technology.

2

The Imaginary Organization—
Related Theories and
Perspectives*

The concept of the "imaginary organization" serves as a framework for our efforts to understand and integrate several previous observations, concepts, and theories from business research and practice. It is probably easiest to speak of a *perspective* on business organization, a set of concepts intended to depict the structures and processes which we have observed. However, from a strict methodological point of view, it may be more correct to speak of an approach to a *meta-theory*, a synthesis of different theories which we then apply to what we are studying. In his book *Sensemaking in Organizations*, Karl Weick (1995) expresses an ambition to present "a frame of mind about frames of mind". Our approach could perhaps also be described in this way. Thus, we do not claim to be introducing a new theory of business. On the contrary, it is important for us to relate our model and our concepts as well as possible to theories close to our own, and to central concepts of business administration. In the following discussion, we review some of these building blocks.

COMPANIES IN NETWORKS: COMPANIES AS NETWORKS

An important aspect of the imaginary organization is the cohesion of the network. Theories on networks surrounding companies and

---

* Bo Hedberg is indebted to his students in the research program on Imaginary Organizations, and especially to Henrik Uggla and Jan Torpman, for discussions concerning this frame of reference.

representing their environment began to emerge several decades ago. Prominent leaders in this development were researchers at the University of Uppsala (Jan Johansson, Håkan Håkansson, and others) and at the Stockholm School of Economics (Lars-Gunnar Mattsson). Their research, sometimes referred to as "the Uppsala School", has received considerable attention, and in several respects it has shifted the focus of research and our understanding of market, communication and the relationship between a company and its environment. At the outset, the Uppsala researchers concentrated on industrial marketing. The following statement is representative of their thinking in the early 1980s:

> Building up a company's connections with the market requires a long-term effort. And afterwards the company must keep working at maintaining and developing them. This effort is an investment. At many companies such market investments are the most important ones of all. Connections in industrial markets constitute a network of vital importance for the competitiveness of the company. The market network both sets the limits and furnishes the opportunities for the company's development. (Hägg & Johansson, 1982).

In focusing on the company's interaction with sophisticated industrial customers, the "network researchers" emphasized the long-term nature of the relationships which had developed, as well as the loyalty within them. While contemporary books on marketing employed the imagery of a market war—the battle for market share, and picking the right artillery, or "marketing mix"—the Uppsala researchers described how companies, by viewing not only their sales markets but also their purchasing markets (purchasing relationships) as interactions in networks, can use their understanding to build up solid and enduring relationships which benefit many actors in the long run (Hammarkvist et al, 1982).

Today it is clear that many of the findings from studies of actors in industrial markets (business-to-business) can also be applied to markets in faster moving items, in services, and in consumer goods (Moss Kanter, 1994). For example, creating long-term customer loyalty is a primary purpose of grocery stores, hotel chains, gasoline stations, and the customer clubs of banks and mail-order companies; IKEA's "Family concept" is an early illustration. Then, by using shopping cards and offering customer benefits, companies often attempt to create from these primary customer habits a network of interacting businesses under their own management or in collaboration with partners, sometimes referred to as value-added networks.

The Uppsala school is based on a systems approach in which an understanding of the concept as a whole, positioning, dynamics, and interaction are central elements. In this tradition, a rather sharp distinction is drawn between the company (the internal system) and its environment (the external system of markets for selling, obtaining resources, and competition).

Our concept of the imaginary organization includes network theories as an important element. But, unlike the Uppsala school, we do not find it natural to distinguish between the "company" and its "environment". The imaginary organizations which we have studied tend to regard the entire playing field as the "company" when building up new businesses, or to view virtually all parts of their current operation as a potential "environment" when renovating old ones.

Furthermore, the imaginary organizations which we describe are held together not only by purchasing and selling relationships but by other cohesive forces, like co-ordinating information, an attractive culture, and a common concept of business for the entire system constituting the imaginary organization.

LOOSELY COUPLED SYSTEMS AND ADHOCRACIES

Weick (1979) described educational organizations as "loosely coupled systems". These systems also have numerous points of contact with the imaginary organizations as we observed them in our studies. Weick speaks of systems in which management by objectives is neither so direct nor so mechanical as conventional management literature suggests. Co-ordination is not equally close throughout the system. Certain parts may be more tightly interlinked, others less so. "A sensitive sensing mechanism" is needed to hold the system together. Much of the necessary learning and mutual adaptation take place locally, and in subsystems. A "technical core" can constitute a central coupling element. Around this core different building blocks and subsystems can be arranged in a fashion that facilitates mutation and innovative learning.

Charles Handy (1989) noted the revival of federative organizations: "Federalism implies a variety of individual groups allied together under a common flag with some shared identity. Federalism seeks to make it big by keeping it small, or at least independent, by combining autonomy with co-operation". Handy then proceeds to describe his concept, the *shamrock organization*. The shamrock consists of: (1) *the professional core*; (2) *the contractual fringe*; (3) *the flexible labor force*; and (4) *the consumers (prosumers)* who participate in the creation of value through self-service, feedback, word-of-mouth, etc. Clearly, Handy has seen the same kinds of enterprises as those we describe in this book. Management at Skandia AFS, as a matter of fact, usually describe their company as a federative organization, and the shamrock terminology could no doubt be used to characterize AFS.

Mintzberg (1983) ended his book on organizational structures by identifying the *adhocracy*. In a later book *Mintzberg on Management* (Mintzberg, 1989) he renames adhocracy and talks about the *innovative organization* which is characterized by co-ordination through mutual adjustment and where major design parameters are, among others, liaison devices, organic structure, selective decentralization, and horizontal job specialization. In the innovative organization (adhocracy) "specialists are typically grouped into functional units for housekeeping purposes" but they are actually "deployed in small market-based project teams to do their work". The adhocracy (innovative organization) shares many characteristics with our IO-patterns although the former apparently are still seen as one company. In the later book Mintzberg (1989) moves on to identify two additional structural patterns; the *ideological (missionary) organization* and the *political organization*. The ideological organization is one where ideologies, traditions, and sagas play important roles as coordinators of action, and where visibly loosely coupled systems are glued together through the sharing of visions, missions, and beliefs between the members. Ideology and a strong sense of mission play an important role in several of the imaginary organizations which we will visit later in this book.

SERVICE MANAGEMENT, RELATIONSHIP MARKETING

While it has long been realized that service companies and producers of goods do not have the same problems, service companies and their problems were given a clearer profile in Richard Normann's (1984) book *Service Management*. Normann emphasizes the ephemeral nature of a service, the importance of the delivery system for services, and the concept of the customer base. He describes service systems and "innovative linking of human resources" and develops a model of Service Management Systems with five principal components:

1. The market segment
2. The service concept
3. The service delivery system, with three subcomponents— personnel, the customer, and technology and physical support
4. The image
5. Culture and philosophy.

Research on service businesses has since developed considerably; examples include the work of Grönroos (1990) and Gummesson (1995) in Finland and Sweden, respectively. Together with a number of other researchers in the Nordic countries, they have laid the foundation for what has been referred to with increasing frequency as The Nordic School of Service Management.

There is a considerable overlap in many respects between the ideas central to service management and those relevant to the imaginary organization. The focus is on the creation of value for the customer, who is often himself involved in creating this value. Successful service companies design composite services which are co-ordinated, bundled, and packaged to achieve the best market effect. Systems of production units, delivery systems, customer bases, and arrangements for quality assurance are built up. Companies in networks (value-added networks, or VANs) collaborate in this process. The similarities between the conceptual world of research in service management and the imaginary organizations which we describe become even more apparent when we compare the recent work of Wikström et al (*Knowledge and Value*, 1994) and some of Gummesson's publications (1995, 1996). There is every reason to believe that these advances will prove mutually fruitful to an even greater extent in the future.

The majority of the imaginary organizations which we have studied up to now are more or less pure service enterprises, but some of them are also producers or suppliers of goods which include a substantial element of service. However, *the customer base, value creation, delivery system,* and *core competence* are always important in the imaginary organization. Our conclusion is that one of the main purposes of the imaginary organization is precisely to form an *organization based on the customer and the market.* The impulse for learning comes from the customer, the scarce resource, who has the power to choose, or not to choose, the company's products. The farther we go from the market and the closer we get to the system of production, the more we are likely to find that the IO company has purchased freedom of action and flexibility by using partnership to assure itself of the necessary resources. One might outline the images of the imaginary organization and of relationship marketing as two maps showing the same ground from two different points of origin (see Figure 2.1). It is also clear that the ideas of a company's *production of knowledge* and of its *learning,* in contact with the customer in the marketplace or in the systems of delivery

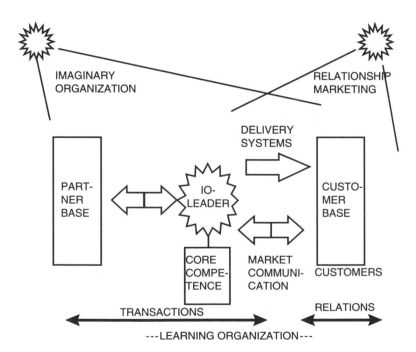

Figure 2.1 Imaginary organization and relationship marketing—two perspectives

and production, are intimately related to a meta-theory of imaginary organization.

"The knowledge-intensive firm" (KIF) became the focus of interest in Scandinavian research and discourse on management in the 1980s. Sveiby & Risling (1986) wrote a management text that headed the list of top sellers in Sweden for years. The message was clear and simple: many modern firms possess little but knowledge, and they grow and thrive from their excellence in monitoring and securing the knowledge-creation process. As a consequence, they face difficulties when compiling their balance sheets, and their leaders face new challenges in attracting knowledge workers to the company. Banks find it difficult to grant loans, and stock markets keep their distance. Many imaginary organizations are KIFs, or at least they share many of the same problems when it comes to interacting with the business world of today.

LEARNING ORGANIZATIONS—COMPANIES AS INTERACTING PROCESSES

The perspective of the "knowledge-intensive firm" is of course very close to the idea of the company as a learning organization. Much of the research on learning organizations has shown how companies that have done well become prisoners of their own success, losing more and more of their learning capacity the longer their success continues (Hedberg et al, 1976). Countless organizations have found it difficult, and sometimes impossible, to go from single-loop learning to double-loop learning (Argyris, & Schön, 1978).

To see organizations as arrangements of processes (Weick, 1979; Forrester, 1961; Nyström et al, 1976), and to design systems to maintain flexibility and curiosity (Box & Draper, 1969; Campbell, 1969; Hedberg & Jönsson, 1978), can be a way to keep the process of learning alive. Perhaps a more general answer to this set of problems is the idea of the "client-driven enterprise", of linking the internal processes of the organization closely to the customers that constitute the market. Virtually all of the companies which we describe in this book as imaginary organizations are quite clearly "client-driven" and live very close to the market and to customer processes of value creation.

After these attempts at comparing and contrasting the imaginary organization with similar concepts and schools of theory, it may be appropriate to present briefly certain theoretical approaches which may prove important for adding to our understanding of how imaginary organizations can be co-ordinated and led. Theories of transaction costs belong to the former group. Hirschman's (1970) model of "exit, voice and loyalty" (see below) is highly relevant to the question of how to retain personnel and maintain their commitment in loosely coupled organizations and networks. Later in the book we will also show how our set of concepts relates to questions concerning a company's core competence and to the concept of outsourcing.

THE TRANSACTION-COST APPROACH—EXCHANGING HIERARCHY FOR CO-ORDINATION BY IT

Classical organization theorists used to debate—sometimes quite vigorously—the question of the "span of control", or the appropriate number of employees reporting to a single manager. As systems and techniques of control became more refined, the theoretical optimum increased. With today's modern information technology (LAN, groupware, Internet, etc.), the transaction costs of organizational co-ordination drop so sharply that at a number of new points hierarchy can be replaced by the market.

The transaction-cost approach was developed by Williamson (1975, 1981) and was originally and most brilliantly formulated in 1937 by Ronald H. Coase, winner of the Nobel Prize in economics, in a very concise article named *The Nature of the Firm*. Here, Coase describes how the choice between hierarchy and the market may be understood in terms of relative prices based on transaction cost. The cost of co-ordination must be balanced against the cost of assuring efficiency. The market is preferable when the cost of co-ordination is relatively low and competition leads to high efficiency, but hierarchy is often the only economically feasible solution to the problem of co-ordination. In a world in which modern information technology is radically enlarging the possibilities of co-ordination and thus greatly reducing transaction costs, one should also expect a dramatic shift from hierarchy to market.

We may assume that imaginary organizations can often emerge when transaction costs decline to the point where effective co-ordination becomes possible with a minimum of traditional hierarchy. Lateral co-ordination of the core competence of partner enterprises by internal market forces replaces the co-ordination which was previously provided, through necessity or force of habit, by a hierarchy.

The system constituted by the imaginary organization may thus be viewed as an internal market for the IO enterprise; favorable terms of exchange between the leader enterprise and partner enterprises create an efficient trade in competence and resources, so that the business as a whole becomes more competitive than it could have been if co-ordinated by a hierarchy.

DOING BUSINESS AS A CHAIN ENTERPRISE AND IN FRANCHISING SYSTEMS

Chain enterprises are enterprises in which a common concept of business, a physical infrastructure, and/or a joint purchasing organization or competence in marketing is used by a number of similar companies. Co-ordination among the companies in the chain may be voluntary or based on some form of ownership. In the latter case, the ownership relates to the shared infrastructure. If the concept of business and the brand name are more distinct and explicit, we are talking about a franchising system. The owner of the franchising concept makes it available to a number of franchise holders under a contract which requires them to pay a fee and to submit to comprehensive regulation. McDonalds may be the best-known example of successful world-wide franchising.

Imaginary organizations may be designed as chains. They may also be built around a franchising concept. But the "company" consists of the business as a whole, and relations between actors include the kind of synergies that make the whole greater than the sum of its parts. Simply "cloning" a successful company into a number of separate copies will hardly create a basis for an imaginary organization. What definitely will, however, is sharing a concept of business more widely, arranging a network of partners, and establishing a joint logistics system (EDI) or a system of delivery on demand within an otherwise federated organization. Here, while it will probably be necessary to specify the boundaries of the imaginary organization, it should be emphasized that the imaginary organization is primarily a perspective on doing business.

In some cases, imaginary organizations may also bear a striking resemblance to some of the more intricate corporate structures which we find. Particularly when it comes to developing existing companies in the direction of a more imaginary architecture and strategy, imaginary organizations can surely find a place within corporate structures like that of Asea Brown Boveri (ABB).

EXIT, VOICE, LOYALTY—VISION AND TRUST

The very title of Hirschman's (1970) classical book, *Exit, Voice and Loyalty*, reveals the essence of his model—one of mechanisms which promote efficiency in companies (as well as in the public sector). Management is dependent on feedback from both the company and its environment in order to maintain and improve the company's efficiency and adaptive capacity.

If the mechanisms which promote efficiency are to work, there must be a certain degree of loyalty. Employees must care enough about how the company is doing to consider its welfare and get involved in its future. If they do, they may then send signals in an effort to influence management. However, loyalty should be sufficient but not excessive. If loyalty knows no bounds, management may not bother to listen. If it is lacking, staff may be too quick to leave the enterprise instead of trying to change it. If the enterprise is held together by the right degree of loyalty, personnel will have two ways to inform management of their discontent or to propose change: "*exit*" and "*voice*". An employee (or other involvee) may resort to "*voice*"—the system of information, meetings, etc.—to gain the attention of management. If he/she is unable to do so, or if results in the desired direction are not forthcoming, the "*exit*" option remains: he/she can leave the enterprise. Exit and voice are ways of putting pressure on management to change.

One would think that the same mechanisms would also be present in the relationship of the enterprise to its environment. Customers can protest, demanding better service ... or they can turn their back on the enterprise and patronize the competition. Suppliers and partners may react in a similar manner, with exit and voice in a framework of functional loyalty (see Figure 2.2).

It is interesting to apply Hirschman's model to the systems which we call imaginary organizations. Here, the challenge to management is to instill sufficient loyalty among collaborating islands of enterprise. A perhaps large number of people who are involved, while not employees, must be made to care about what happens to the business as a whole. The management of the leader enterprise may truly have to present a clear image of objectives, an exciting, unifying *vision*, for the *entire* imaginary organization. Similarly, the challenge of listening to voice applies throughout the system. To permit exit, while not making it too easy, poses a number of problems for management:

- How useful is the competence of the partner/individual outside of the imaginary organization?
- How can joint know-how be codified and collected in the form of structural capital?

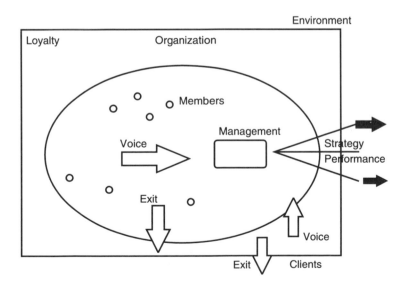

Figure 2.2 Exit, voice, and loyalty (Hirschman's model)

- How important is it that there be alternatives on the market?
- Where are the critical relationships of dependence in the imaginary organization?

But before resort is made to exit, voice should have been tried. Naturally, the opposite sequence is hardly possible. Therefore, the leaders of imaginary organizations should carefully consider:

- The availability of channels of communication and forums for criticism and suggestions.
- Their own attentiveness to what the involvees are trying to say.
- The importance of being able to articulate and verbalize the need for change.
- The need for multiple arenas of interaction within the system.
- A set of values which in word and deed underscores the desirability of dialogue and diversity.

Hirschman's original empirical findings were taken from government bureaucracies and large manufacturing companies. One would expect that in knowledge-intensive companies the conditions for exercising voice and exit would be somewhat different. Here many employees are used to expressing themselves, and they expect others to listen. At the same time, the barriers to leaving, at least the physical ones, are low; the employee simply takes his capital with him. There is a great need for leadership which formulates *visions*, which engenders and reinforces a sense that the work is *meaningful*, and which can inspire loyalty to the business.

Probably these challenges (and problems) exist to an even higher degree in those businesses to which we refer here as imaginary organizations. There are many opportunities for exit. The structure for transmitting voice is different. And the mechanisms which underlie loyalty can be complex.

A final, and very important mechanism to keep imaginary organizations together goes through the building of *trust*. Management in Skandia AFS talk and write of their organization using the concept of "High-trust culture". And the concept of trust is getting increasingly interesting to researchers who study federative organizations and other systems where mutual adjustment takes place repeatedly in dynamic and organically growing organizations. When trust is threatened, imaginary organizations may rapidly fall apart, as the example of Hemglass illustrates.

Hemglass

Hemglass (Home Icecream) is a case which illustrates how vulnerable an imaginary organization can be when partners begin to exit and when previously established trust is lost. Hemglass AB was founded in 1968 by Eric Ericsson, an enterprising dairyman and chemical engineer. Ericsson's interest centered on the product itself, ice cream (the name "Hemglass" may be translated as "home-delivered ice cream"). Quality was a key word for him; the ice cream had to be and taste fresh on the tongue of the consumer. To assure quality, Ericsson wanted to establish an unbroken chain of refrigeration. In this chain from the plant to the consumer, however, the distribution of the ice cream was a weak link. To strengthen it, he conceived the idea of ice-cream delivery trucks. The Hemglass distribution system was more the product of a chemical engineer's and ice-cream lover's thinking than that of a franchiser–engineer. But the result was ... an imaginary organization.

The production of ice cream ran smoothly, and a rather loosely coupled sales organization was gradually established to increase sales. Ericsson remained interested mostly in production and product development. Abounding in ambition but lacking in capital, he was able to line up an increasing number of independent salesmen with trucks to distribute from the ice-cream plant. In time the concept became extremely successful. Hemglass turned into a profit machine which attracted the interest of new investors. Ericsson sold out.

In the early 1990s the Hemglass trend of continuing success was broken. Previous years of profit were followed by years of losses. Both efficiency and product development had been neglected. A new managing director was brought in, first as a consultant and then on a permanent basis just before still another change of ownership. The new managing director streamlined production, put some life into product development and quality improvement, and stepped up the pressure on the sales force. The results were by and large successful, but it became apparent that the sales force had been pushed a little too hard. Late in the autumn of 1992, a very large proportion of

Hemglass' independent salesmen announced that they were leaving Hemglass to start a competing company, Glassbilen (transl: the ice-cream truck), in collaboration with a major Finnish producer of ice cream. Soon every block was visited by two similar ice-cream trucks, distinguishable primarily by the shade of their blue paint and the musical jingle played over their loudspeaker. Hemglass was facing a rugged challenge. Customers had been offered an alternative right on the nearest corner.

While assuming and developing its role as a capable and efficient producer of ice cream, Hemglass had clearly failed to secure the allegiance of its customers. And it had no way of controlling its sales force. Another producer tried to take over the imaginary organization. In haste Hemglass was forced to concentrate on saving what it could and then building up a partially new network of salesmen with new trucks.

Even back in his days as a dairyman, Ericsson had put himself in a rather vulnerable position in the IO enterprise centered around Hemglass. Customer contact was in the hands of the ice-cream truck owners, and the customer base consisted of a very large number of small, individual units spread out along the routes served by the trucks. The retail link grew organically, without any clear structure or organization. During the entire period from 1968 through 1979, there was no contract between Hemglass and the truck owners. And even after a contract had been reached, it was mostly just a printed version of the practices which had been developed in the business over the previous 10 years or so.

The retailers themselves were a heterogeneous group which varied considerably in size, selling ability, solvency, and efficiency. Early on, some of the major truck owners began to regard Ericsson and his Hemglass as a mere supplier, not as a leading actor in a system of partnership. They viewed the system differently and had little commitment in support of the business as a whole. Thus, conflicting objectives were built into the system: for Hemglass the profitability of the plant was most important; for the retailers, it was the profit to be made on distribution.

The weaknesses of the imaginary organization became apparent, and gradually people began to leave. New owners and a new, professional management took over in January 1992. The latter turned the spotlight on the quality of distribution and made their views and requirements known to the sales force. Management demands that the salesmen consider the interests of the business as a whole led to increasing tension in their relationship. In less than a year the crisis broke out: nearly half the sales force took their trucks, repainted them with the Glassbilen colors and logo, and joined forces with the Finnish ice-cream producer. The market war escalated. The delivery schedules of Hemglass were much sought after by their rival, which tried to reach each stopping point just ahead of them.

A little more than a year later, Glassbilen folded, and most of the salesmen returned to Hemglass. The market was too small for both of them, and the Finnish supplier had grown tired of the quarreling and found new growth markets in neighboring countries of Eastern Europe.

The case of Hemglass illustrates how important it is for the leading actor to own the relationship with the customer, and for the imaginary organization to provide clearly perceived synergies and set common objectives. If the interaction of the parties is viewed simply as a buyer/seller relationship, and if objectives are diffuse and conflicting, there is probably only one possible outcome if the system is put under stress.

SUMMARY

The perspective of the imaginary organization may be seen as a meta-perspective based on a conception of organizations, and markets, as networks, and of loosely coupled systems which co-ordinate arrangements of organizational processes. Between processes there are transactions, and over time relationships are developed. The enterprise begins with the market, with the customers' process of value creation, and works backwards through the system of delivery to the system of production. The latter consists of a core—the leader enterprise with its core competence—and a number of partners who on a more or less permanent basis collaborate in the functions of production and delivery to the market. In co-ordination and in the learning process of the system as a whole, information technology plays a major role which is rapidly becoming even greater. Traditional boundaries between the firm and its environment, between what is within the firm and what is outside it, between the market and the internal organization (hierarchy), are disappearing,

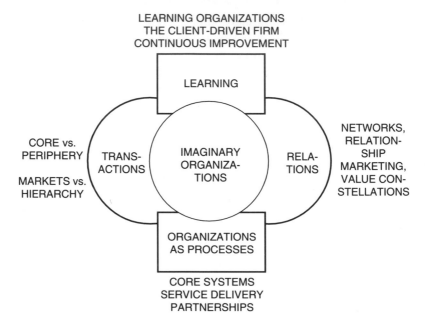

Figure 2.3 Imaginary organizations and some related concepts

and the various subsystems are becoming part of each other (Figure 2.3).

In summary, service enterprises, chains of enterprises, and imaginary organizations have many points in common, and there are a number of related theories and fragments of theories which may prove important for anticipating and understanding the problems which can arise in imaginary organizations.

3

Patterns of Creation, Renovation, and Extension

The purpose of this chapter and of Chapters 4–8 is to summarize a number of *patterns* and *structures* found in the case studies on which we have based our presentation. A selection of these case studies is presented in greater detail in the Appendix. We have chosen to distinguish between patterns for creating new imaginary organizations, and patterns for renovation and extension of existing companies with the aid of an IO perspective. There is undoubtedly some overlap between the two categories.

PATTERNS FOR CREATION

We started out with certain clear ideas about a number of possible patterns for creating an imaginary organization; an entrepreneur might choose any of them on its own merits. However, only one pattern emerges clearly from our case studies: the distinguishing feature of every constellation which we have been able to observe and describe has been the *spider web*.

The spider web

The *spider web* is a pattern in which a company (the leader enterprise) takes the lead in building an imaginary organization by involving, contracting with, or inspiring other companies and actors to collaborate in a specific business venture directed at a specific market. The original IO-leader belongs to the leader enterprise, which formulates a concept of the business, builds up a circle of customers, often establishes networks for production and distribution, and sometimes even arranges a system for payment. While the extent of the "spider's" activities may vary, the leader enterprise is always an indispensable element of the imaginary organization which has been created.

The other elements, which are centered around the leader enterprise or "spider", are a customer base, a partner base, the special competence of the leader enterprise, and one or more systems to co-ordinate sales, co-operation among the partners, and production. These key elements may be summarized as follows:

- Customer base.
- The base of the leader enterprise (core competence).
- Partner base.
- Delivery systems.
- Production systems (including quality control and logistics).
- Payment systems.
- Communication systems.

A somewhat stylized representation of the "spider web" itself is shown in Figure 3.1.

Among our case studies, the following show the spider-web pattern: Scandinavian PC Systems, Lorentzen & Wettre, the Stockholm Stock Exchange, GANT, Liber–Hermods, Folkoperan (transl: People's Opera), Grammofon AB Bis, IMIT, Kalmarsalen,

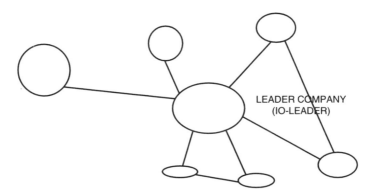

Figure 3.1   The imaginary system (the spider in the web)

SCF (transl: Swedish Association of School of Economics Graduates), and the Värmdö Municipal Office of Cultural Affairs (Värmdö kommuns kultursekretariat).

Interconnected islands

Spider webs may differ considerably. One variety may be termed *"interconnected islands"* (Figure 3.2). In this pattern, one or several companies seek to join forces with similar enterprises so as to achieve economies of scale, geographic coverage, an effective infrastructure, etc., and thus render the whole greater than the sum of its parts. This pattern is based on collaboration among different parties, and on their common perception of synergies in one or more phases of the process of value creation. Chain stores and co-operating travel agencies may serve as examples. Thus, Rosenbluth International, a Texas travel enterprise, took the initiative in building up a network of collaborating but independent travel agencies. While each agency operates locally and regionally, a jointly owned global communications system permits them to function together as a world-wide travel agency, with resources, representation, and local connections everywhere. Our case study of IMIT resembles this pattern in many respects.

United front toward the market

The *"united front toward the market"* is another spider-web pattern, in which a company establishes a trade mark, a concept, a customer

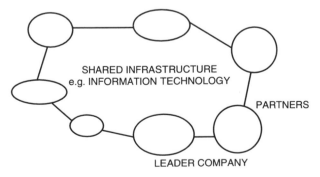

Figure 3.2 Interconnected islands

base, or some other unifying factor, and then engages other parties, in collaboration or by purchasing arrangements, to produce and distribute goods or services. The classic cottage industries were designed this way, as are McDonald's and certain other franchising systems. So are modern suppliers of ready-to-wear clothing like GANT (Pyramid Sportswear AB), In-Wear, Martinique, and Lapidus. Another example is Pappersgruppen, the joint sales company for the paper products of the Swedish paper mills Papyrus, Billerud, and some minor mills. Many years ago, Pappersgruppen set up an excellent system of market communications which served as a link between the old paper companies and their industrial customers. A market information system, PISTOL (Product Information SysTem On-Line), made it possible to improve the level of customer service substantially. Afterwards, the order function of the system was actually transferred to major customers (Figure 3.3). This strategy was subsequently followed by the wholesale company Luna AB toward hardware stores, and later still by Basket InfoLink for other chain stores.

Initially, we had also identified a pattern of co-operation which we called "the clockwork", in which the imaginary organization consisted of a number of components closely intermeshing like the cogwheels of a clock. Each component performed a vital function in

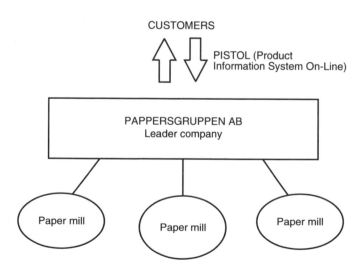

Figure 3.3 A united front toward the market

the operation of the mechanism—in this case, getting the product to the customer. One example, described in *Business Week*, involved voluntary co-operation among several professional craftsmen to produce one of the highest-quality kayaks in the world. However, this particular pattern was conspicuously absent from our case studies.

The missing link

The *missing link* is a somewhat different pattern in which a company finds and develops a specialty, or niche, which complements a previous system and vastly improves its functioning. The contribution of the missing link is often to reduce transaction costs or improve market information so that an existing market can be reached and be made to grow. In this situation the role of the leader enterprise is often that of a broker between the markets of supply and demand, and the point of the imaginary concept is to reduce transaction costs to a level that makes market trading economically attractive. *Gula Tidningen*, a Stockholm-area newspaper containing only classified ads, is one example of this kind. Another is CompUStore, which has successfully established itself in the USA, Norway, and several other countries as a lowest-price data base for various forms of durable goods. CompUStore sells "lowest-available-price information" to its subscribers, often as part of some other customer benefit, such as the VIP privileges granted by a bank or insurance company. CompUStore has built up an effective computerized system which at all times can provide current information on the lowest available market price of white goods, electronic equipment, and other items. The customer may telephone the company to find out the price of some item and then go and buy it at a local store. Or he may buy the item directly from CompUStore, which obtains it from a co-operating dealer (perhaps the customer's own neighborhood store) and in the evening has it sent to the customer's home by a co-operating express-delivery chain.

The missing-link company plays an important part in the functioning of the new market, but it also competes with other market channels or with the producers themselves. Consequently, the system is relatively vulnerable.

We find a potential missing-link pattern when we examine the various parties in Sweden with an interest in efficient systems of payment. The technical solution of a "petty-cash" card—an inexpensive "smart card" programmed for a certain sum of money which can be drawn on for minor payments in cases where change and small bills otherwise would have been used—has been available for over 10 years. Telia, the Swedish national telephone company, has introduced the cards for use in pay telephones, but broader, more general applications remain unexploited. Kontocentralen (the charge-account center jointly owned by the Swedish Postal service, Telia, the banks, the Retail Trade Association, and a number of charge-card companies), is presently studying the question of how and where a Swedish petty-cash card might be introduced. But at least so far, it appears that the missing link is still missing—the components are there, but the leader enterprise is not.

In summary, all constellations which we have found in our case-study companies, as well as all systems which we have encountered in the literature and other available reports, are basically varieties of the spider-web pattern.

PATTERNS FOR RENOVATION AND EXTENSION

When it comes to patterns for renovation and extension of existing companies from an IO perspective, the variety is much greater. Here we can identify the following principal patterns, or—more properly—strategies.

Share a customer base

This pattern is built on the foundation of a good, solid customer base. The strategy for development is to create additional value, or to provide additional services, for existing customers. Other actors are invited to participate in customer communication. Svenska Pressbyrån, a chain of news-stands, underwent the change described in our case study. Another example taken from our case studies is that of Fritzes, a publisher of legislation and other official regulations. All the while maintaining its customer relationships with government agencies and its "know-*who*" in the form of long-standing contacts with experts in law, medicine, taxation, and other fields, Fritzes lost no time in setting up an imaginary organization to meet the CD-Rom challenge (see Figure 3.4).

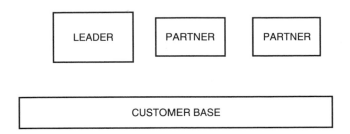

Figure 3.4 A pattern for renovation: share a customer base

Share delivery systems

This is a pattern in which the delivery system provides a solid foundation for enlarging the range of goods or services offered. One example is the alliance between national postal services in several countries and banks, insurance companies, or mortgage providers that need the post offices as service delivery systems towards mass markets. Another example is provided by the book-publishing and travel-agency operations of certain daily newspapers. The Svenska Pressbyrån, cited above, is of course also based on its extensive network of news-stands, which make it a very attractive delivery system (see Figure 3.5).

Share production facilities

Here the critical resource is a superior product or production process. The company can be useful to several product developers or serve as

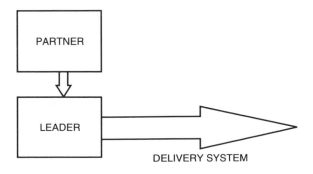

Figure 3.5 A pattern for renovation: share delivery systems

a supplier to several delivery systems. For a long time, newspapers often, in pairs, have jointly owned or otherwise shared printing facilities, even when their respective editorial positions and advertising policies have differed sharply. Most confectioners manufacture candy in bulk for ultimate purchase by the piece; then the candy is sold through other delivery systems independent of the confectioners' brands. Many, though not all, of the recent out-sourcing arrangements for company computer operations and systems development have followed the same pattern: a deliberately implemented strategic renovation of an existing company (see Figure 3.6).

Share our image

While the *shared image* resembles the entrepreneurial pattern of the *united front toward the market*, it may be considered an extension as well as a renovation. The management of a mature, even stagnant business concludes that the brand name, reputation, situation, or market position is virtually all that remains from a by-gone era of glory. Outside entrepreneurs are invited to bring in new dynamism under a shared image. A good example is the successful transformation of the NK department store in Stockholm (see Figure 3.7). The prestigious downtown department store had become stagnant, and the staff were rather high-brow and arrogant. In order to shop here, one had to go home and dress impressively before hand so as to be

Figure 3.6 A pattern for renovation: share production facilities

INDEPENDENT SHOPS
SHARED INFRASTRUCTURE

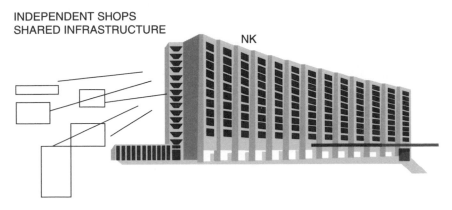

Figure 3.7 A pattern for renovation: share our image

able to pass the scrutiny of the NK assistants. The recipe for renewal was simple and straightforward; get rid of the current staff and of the NK culture and bring in new entrepreneurs and customer-pleasing staff. Thus, an number of imaginary organizations such as GANT, Boomerang, Peak Performance, Calida, etc. moved in and gathered under the NK umbrella . The positive parts of the old NK image were combined with the dynamism of the new actors and their much more motivated staff.

4

Examples of Successful Creation, Renovation, and Extension

In a constantly changing business environment, new opportunities and threats are always arising. These situations are handled in various ways, depending on the positions and frames of reference of the parties involved. In this chapter we present a number of case studies in which management has successfully responded to challenge by using an IO perspective. Usually a principal figure has acted as "imaginator" (see Chapter 1), although of course without referring to him/herself as such or even thinking in those terms. As we have stated, the imaginary organization is a perspective on business rather than a newly invented form of organization. We must make visible the invisible if we are to find the right course of action. That is why we present our case studies at this point, before we turn to the subject of managing and leading an imaginary organization.

The case studies were chosen to inspire managers to think more in imaginary terms, and also to show that solutions based on an IO approach have been and can be reached in many different settings—in large operations as well as small ones; in private business and in the public sector; in the traditional industries of manufacturing and commerce as well as in areas which we do not consider part of the business world, such as the theater and professional interest groups. In cases of the latter type, the IO perspective may have been adopted because a lack of resources made it necessary to try a new approach. Since we believe that present developments in our society will make similar solutions attractive in mature industries and the public sector as well, we have also included some examples from these categories. In other literature we find detailed accounts of co-operation in strategic development between major industrial companies; here, too, an imaginary organization can be said to exist.

One reason why there are not more examples from industry is that this sector currently accounts for a rather modest share of total employment in Sweden, a fact that does not otherwise emerge very clearly from management literature. While the imaginary organization may indeed be appropriate for manufacturing companies, as our examples show, we should perhaps expect it to be most widespread among newly created enterprises in the service sector.

We have classified our case studies according to the key words which we used in the previous chapter: creation, renovation, and extension. They differ from each other in that IO thinking has proved helpful in different kinds of situations. In the *creation* of a new enterprise, the imaginator puts together the imaginary organization which he has envisioned (the spider weaves its web). *Renovation* is appropriate when an existing organization is run down and no longer works. Certain parts must be replaced. Thinking in IO terms can help management to determine an appropriate division of functions and to recruit new partners.

When a company is performing satisfactorily but management is looking for growth or product improvement, an *extension* may be appropriate. In this case the IO perspective is most useful for taking stock of the resources in the network. The leader enterprise can diagnose the respective needs and competence of suppliers and customers and, by exercising more active control, make them partners. In some cases of extension, an element of renovation is present; it may be necessary to replace an existing partner with a new one better adapted to the higher level of ambition which prompted the extension.

The reader may want to concentrate on certain case studies which particularly attract his interest. In the Appendix we provide background data on most of the companies studied. These companies are indicated in **bold** type in the list below. In Chapter 8 we will continue our discussion by drawing conclusions from all of the cases. Before then we will comment on the following examples:

Creations: **Grammofon AB Bis**
               Folkoperan (transl: People's Opera),
               Kalmarsalen
               IMIT (Institute for Management of Innovation
               and Technology)

Renovations: **Svenska Pressbyrån** (transl: Swedish Press
               Bureau)

               SCF (Svenska Civilekonomföreningen; transl:
               Swedish Association of School of Economics
               Graduates)
               Lorentzen & Wettre

Extensions: **The Värmdö Municipal Office of Cultural
               Affairs** (Värmdö kommuns kultursekretariat)
               SATT CONTROL
               Alfa Laval Agri Manure Business
               Lord's
               The Stockholm Stock Exchange (Stockholms
               Fondbörs)
               CE Fritzes

In the following three chapters we will examine the various examples and thereafter summarize our observations. The Appendix also provides additional information on some of the other case studies to which we refer in the text.

5

Creation

In two of our examples of creation, new businesses were started with virtually no financial capital. A conventional approach would have found a financial barrier to entry. A strategic development plan for BIS or Folkoperan would have identified a need for resources and translated it into requirements for staffing and financing that could not be met. Barriers like these can be circumvented by starting on a limited scale and obtaining what is needed in co-operation with other parties. In the two examples cited above, there was surely some kind of development plan, but the imaginators realized that being able to *use* resources, rather than owning them, was the essential point.

For our two other examples of creation, KalmarSalen and IMIT, not even a conventional approach would have suggested the establishment of fully-fledged companies with all essential functions under one roof. In these cases the fundamental concept was the role of broker, or intermediary. Still, a number of questions remained: who should do what, which functions should be located in the leader enterprise, how to manage the network of contacts, etc. (All case studies cited in this chapter are presented in greater detail in the Appendix.)

STARTING FROM SCRATCH—STRATEGIES FOR ENTREPRENEURS WITH NO CAPITAL

Many people dream of starting their own business. But the dream usually evaporates when the entrepreneur finds that he lacks the necessary resources. Often he fails to realize that the resources and competence of others can be part of the business. The IO perspective helps the entrepreneur to see opportunities and potential value in what might otherwise appear worthless. It shows that the entrepreneur need only contribute part of the value created for the customer.

Two of our case studies show what can be done by entrepreneurs with limited resources of their own: Grammofon AB BIS and Folkoperan.

Grammofon AB BIS

Grammofon AB BIS was founded by Robert von Bahr in 1973 after the difficulty he had experienced in getting established record companies to put out a recording by his wife at that time. He borrowed some money (SEK 30,000), recorded the tape himself, designed the cover and had the first set of records produced. To reach retailers, he went to the Stockholm railway station and copied the telephone numbers of the country's record stores out of telephone books. For distribution in Stockholm he used a baby carriage. That way he could take the records on the bus and subway at no charge; nothing in the regulations said that there had to be a baby in the carriage.

Gradually a few employees joined the enterprise; each year, editions increased in number and became more ambitious and costly to produce. This year BIS has issued nearly 100 CDs, some of which were reissued from LPs. Everything is to come out on CD, regardless of how well the LP version sold. Here are some of the major milestones:

- An LP of the opera singer Birgit Nilsson when BIS was young and unknown. She was attracted by the opportunity to record songs which she had never sung for any international record company (and probably also by von Bahr's enterprising spirit in contacting her). In this way BIS gained international visibility.
- BIS emphasized recording quality and was very particular about its choice of (foreign) company to press the records. Even in the LP days, it was important to maximize the fidelity of the

recording to the extent technically possible. More on the quality of the BIS sound below!

- The decision after only eight or nine years to put out series of the complete works of various composers. The first big name was Sibelius, and the project is still in progress. It also created visibility for the company.

- The decision at an early stage to get into CDs, well before it was obvious that this medium was here to stay. Similarly, BIS has been one of the few companies to put out MiniDiscs and video discs, although not many of these have yet been sold.

Most of what needs to be done is performed by partners: CD production, composition and printing of text supplements, marketing, and local sales. The most important partners are of course the artists, whom BIS has often helped along in their careers. However, BIS refuses to enter any exclusive-rights agreements. The artists must be free. Yet what gives BIS its special profile is apparent to any buyer, largely because of what von Bahr has kept under BIS's roof precisely for that purpose:

- The sound—it must be high-fidelity; thus, the choice of recording location is important. As recently as a couple of years ago, von Bahr was the sole producer and sound technician. Now there are four others.

- Distribution—the stock of records, which is managed by von Bahr and his wife, is within walking distance of their home. It should be possible to supply any item within 24 hours: "Service pays off".

- The catalog—records are never taken out of stock, a guarantee of quality which also benefits the artists. Sometimes the accountants wonder, though ...

- Partners involved in other areas of the enterprise are few, and relationships with them are virtually permanent. Consequently, there is a clear BIS profile in regard to design, articles for sale, and repertory.

No competitor, large or small, has chosen to keep the same functions as BIS under the roof of the leader enterprise. Many put out recordings on license from other producers, or from tapes submitted by the artists. Normally they would not manage the stock of records themselves or keep items in the catalog forever. Some of them have their own production, while others do their own marketing, at least in some countries. Particularly in the last 10 years, dozens of small companies marketing CDs have emerged and thus entered BIS's domain, in some cases even in Sweden. But no enterprise of BIS's small size appears to have achieved a comparable market position, and none has been able to put out recordings at the same rate.

Swedish Folkopera

In the 1970s a number of free theater groups were formed, some of them with Music theater in their repertory. Few of them have survived. None has grown like the Swedish Folkopera.

In 1976, four people with complementary interests and abilities began to work together. Three of them have stayed on for the whole time: the conductor Kerstin Nerbe; her husband, the movie director Claes Fellbom; and the business graduate and singer Staffan Rydén. Kerstin wanted to conduct and had few engagements; Claes had been able to do a few films, some of them for advertising, but had developed an interest in opera; Staffan wanted to perform parts but was also a talented administrator—today he is the managing director.

The group started out doing tours as a small ensemble. Today the Swedish Folkopera enjoys the status of city theater, and in some years its box-office receipts have equalled those of the Royal Opera. In the beginning these receipts covered 80% of costs. As subsidies increased, this figure dropped to 50%, compared to 9% for the Royal Opera.

Early goals of the Swedish Folkopera were the first theater of its own on Roslagsgatan in Stockholm in 1980, and then, in 1985, the larger theater on Hornsgatan, which it still occupies. Since 1986 there have also been successful guest performances, notably at the Edinburgh Festival. In 1994 there were visits to New York's Brooklyn Academy of Music and to Jerusalem. From the very beginning, the theater has also toured Sweden in collaboration with the Swedish National Touring Theater (Riksteatern). The playbill usually contains certain financial information about the Swedish Folkopera. In recent years the total annual receipts of this extensive operation have been around SEK 30 million. The group has also attracted the attention of researchers; last winter, one from Strathclyde did a full-time job of following Staffan Rydén around for six weeks.

The attic of the building has been made into office space. The coffee shop next to the theater has been taken over and turned into a restaurant. And the group would also like to move into the space in the adjacent building presently occupied by a grocery store.

The three leaders are appointed by the board of the foundation. There are also seven permanent employees as well as three or four on one-year contracts. Other personnel are engaged on a project basis (for a particular production). All told, close to 500 people are involved. On-stage performers are selected by audition; as for the musicians, section leaders are each charged with staffing a particular group of musicians.

This arrangement has worked during all these years in part because Claes and Kerstin also have a sense of administration, and also because Staffan has remained a singer and thus kept in touch with the artistic side of the operation. This fact has also helped him gain the confidence of other artists. The group has thereby been spared the confrontation so often encountered in the theater between artistic ambition oblivious to financial limitations, and administrators with no sense of artistic value.

Formally, the Swedish Folkopera is a corporation owned by a foundation. In addition to the three persons previously mentioned, the corporate board consists of another incorporator, a project manager, and employee representatives. By contrast, the foundation board includes people from the worlds of industry, diplomacy, the theater, etc. Its members have no direct operating responsibilities, but they provide valuable contacts. The foundation board meets twice a year, the corporate board once a month. Subsidies go to the foundation, which in principle may retain them for future years if the corporation is turning a profit at the time. The project as a form of organization is important in that it gives people a sense of involvement. Here, there is a difference between Swedish Folkopera and the Royal Opera. However, a matrix organization, with project managers, has been introduced at the Royal Dramatic Theater.

When Swedish Folkopera moved to new premises, box-office procedures broke down after half a day. Staffan Rydén called the Royal Dramatic Theater, which lent out a person who enjoyed organizing a box office. In six months the job was finished, and the box-office organizer returned to the Royal Dramatic Theater. The same project approach has been taken with the computer system. The idea has been "to look for expertise where you can normally expect to find it".

A number of crisis years in the 1980s left the company insolvent. Another crisis struck in the summer of 1994, when the company was in default and financial reconstruction was required. But the bank stood by the Swedish Folkoperan, reasoning that government subsidies would probably continue, that the operation had shown consistent growth—resulting in ever larger subsidies, and that the company had always met its payments before. When the new theater was about to be acquired in 1985, the group stepped up its search for sponsors, of whom there are now nine. What the group wants is long-term sponsors. The managing director worked very hard to obtain financing from venture-capital companies and nearly succeeded, even though these companies found it hard to understand an operation for which long-term profit was not the primary objective. "Confidence in me as a person is important for obtaining financing," he explained. From the very outset the group has committed itself in writing to the goal that operations be 50% self-financing.

The written statement of goals has remained virtually unchanged since 1976. The starting point has not been availability of resources but what the group has wanted to do. Still, people have found a certain "realism in all the madness". In other words, it has not been, "Since we've got a million, let's do *Carmen*," but "Let's do *Carmen*; we'll need a million" but not two or three million!

However, "building up a company" has been an objective right from the beginning, and while others thought the group should remain a chamber opera on Roslagsgatan, the group saw the move to Hornsgatan as a necessary next step. If that step did not work out, then at least they had tried and could fold, satisfied with what they had accomplished. The same attitude was taken toward the group's first appearance at the Edinburgh Festival; as expected, it left a deficit of SEK 300,000, but it was considered necessary as a test, to face the truth, to see whether the group's recipe for success could work internationally? It did; the following year the group obtained better terms and earned enough to recoup its previous loss. (Both Claes and Staffan have businessmen in their families.)

Structural capital and core know-how

The network of contacts is important. Many artists have been involved on and off in Swedish Folkopera productions, and their contribution has been enriched by what they have learned elsewhere. Over the years the three leaders have developed a store of knowledge about how to solve various problems, and they have continually improved their personal contacts in business and government. Now Staffan no longer has to start by acquainting them with the Swedish Folkopera! All of the three leaders are active in representing the theater. They also try to take turns at meeting the guests of individual sponsor companies. "People like entrepreneurship"—the form of the operation has been an advantage, but it has proven particularly effective always to contact people for a specific purpose rather that just to ask if they could think of some way to help out. Business contacts are well documented. Notes are also taken on performers but are supplemented by recollection: "She auditioned three years ago. Wouldn't she fit the role now?"

What is the distinctive feature of the Swedish Folkopera? What is at the core of its know-how? Some practices are now well known to audiences: the orchestra somewhere behind the singers, translations into modern Swedish, acting with the whole body and in close proximity to the audience. However, in these respects the group has been imitated. Some practices were solutions adopted by necessity (e.g. electronic amplification for an orchestra that was too small up to 1988). For a long time Claes directed almost all productions, thus giving them a particular character. What really makes the Swedish Folkopera special is a kind of atmosphere, intangible, filled with enthusiasm and urgency, intimately related to the form of the project and the personalities of the three central figures. To some degree this special character may be considered part of structural capital (see below). But it is difficult to imagine sharing this formula with other theaters. It has been applied to some extent in Gdansk, but largely because Claes and Kerstin have personally passed their know-how on to others.

USING EXISTING RESOURCES

Many cities and towns have resources like meeting places for various purposes, suppliers of services, hotel rooms, etc., owned and operated by different parties, each of whom tries its best at doing business on its own. During the 1980s it was also common to build large, integrated, multipurpose facilities for exhibitions, concerts, accommodation, etc., even though places of comparable value to customers already existed, waiting for someone to take the initiative in establishing co-operation.

KalmarSalen

One example of such an initiative is KalmarSalen, the hub of a growing visitor and tourist business in Kalmar, a small coastal city in south-eastern Sweden. The business concept is as follows:

> Our business concept is to organize and sell major congresses/conferences/business meetings, as well as events for audiences. KalmarSalen should be an arena for many different kinds of major organized events, a Multi-Purpose Arena.
>
> For congresses and conferences, we offer a complete package: meeting facilities, hotel rooms, meals, transportation, participant administration, and other related arrangements. Our unique competence is to provide an appealing total package, in which we have thought out most of the features in advance but can still add certain options to attract customers. The technical quality of our facilities, like our service, must be outstanding.
>
> The strength of our business lies in the way we run our operation. A small staff of employees takes care of administration. The nature and size of each event determines the degree of services and products to be purchased externally (staff, hotel rooms, transportation, meals, etc.). This way we limit our overhead to a minimum, and we can always provide a tailor-made mix for the customer.

When asked to define the core competence of KalmarSalen, Managing Director Marguerite Nilsson mentioned two factors:

- *Owning its own conference bureau.* This function is critical for "owning" the customer contact and for controlling quality.

- *The co-ordinator.* One of the four permanent employees manages contracts, writes manuals, and is in charge of all co-ordination.

These two central elements enable KalmarSalen to meet with customers, learn about them and from them, build up a store of previous experience, and control quality.

Serving major conferences involves a large number of companies and people external to KalmarSalen. The company, KalmarSalen KB, purchases a number of services and combines them in a package which it sells to the customer. The following are included in the network around KalmarSalen:

- Every hotel in the city of Kalmar and several other hotels in the area.
- Special restaurants.
- The provincial museum (located in the same building; conference programs often feature guided tours).
- Kalmar Castle (museum, assembly rooms, medieval banquets, etc.).
- The glassworks (mouth-blown glass, "hyttsill"—herring dinner, glassworks-style).

The few permanent employees of the leader enterprise offer the customer efficient administration before, during, and after the conference. The following services are provided:

- Project management/consultation—project planning and budgeting, purchase of services, preparation of printed materials, press contacts, exhibition service, and (when required) financing.
- Participant administration—takes care of registration, accommodation, travel planning, etc.
- Budgeting and financial management—a complete financial department in miniature for the customer's conference.

A number of these services are subsequently performed by co-operating consultants and small businesses. But the customer is always dealing one-on-one with KalmarSalen. From start to finish, one of KalmarSalen's project managers is in charge. In addition to the four individuals (equivalent to three full-time employees) at the center of events, 150 people can be involved at mid-conference to assure that participants' meetings, food, leisure time, and rest are provided for.

Naturally, the imaginary organization of KalmarSalen can differ in size and competence depending on the arrangement. In the past year, arrangements included a Social Democratic youth conference (700 participants for one week), a meeting of the commission of the UNESCO council (50 delegates from the Nordic countries), a concentrated course for the Swedish Labor Market Board (film, multislide presentations, and theater), and a one-day conference for the Chamber of Commerce.

Marguerite Nilsson emphasizes that the operation is critically dependent on modern information technology. The register of customers is very important. KalmarSalen has also bought into a databank on future conferences. Direct marketing and administration of conferences in progress require efficient systems. If the system were to be extended further, there would have to be a functioning network that included the conference bureau and the hotels. But all told KalmarSalen has already come a long way in arranging value constellations for differing customer groups.

> Information! That's what it's all about. You have to be extremely clear toward everyone involved to keep the network together and to deliver on your commitments. In an organization like KalmarSalen, you can't just talk and talk and let things develop as they may. You really only get one shot at the target.

The second factor is to a large extent in the hands of the co-ordinator:

> You have to have rules that are clearer than clear. Weekly planning. Standard forms for everything. You have to save time and show that you can act fast, especially when you are dealing with (new) customers. You have to get your offer in without wasting any time and make sure that it's right from the start.

KalmarSalen has also prepared contribution-margin tables so that everyone on the staff can quickly and easily put a deal together and see how it works.

The third factor concerns *creating and building confidence*. A leader must develop and cultivate the network. In particular, Marguerite Nilsson has to activate her "retailers" (local contacts in various organizations, etc.) and provide them with information and sales arguments. Communication is a two-step process. First, "the managing director must work behind the scenes". Then, if KalmarSalen wins the contract for a conference, Marguerite Nilsson often arranges a press conference in which the "retailer" plays the starring role.

It is also essential to keep in close touch with other suppliers. Marguerite Nilsson generally meets with them one at a time so as to create just the right relationship with each. "It is important to be on very good terms with these key people."

When asked to compare her former leadership at Orrefors Glass-works with what is now needed at KalmarSalen, Marguerite Nilsson replied:

1. There has to be a *motor* (with energy, motivation, and persistence) in both cases.
2. You have to be *much more clear* when you are running KalmarSalen. (There is not much chance to correct a mistake.)
3. You have virtually *no employees*. Most of the people working for you are "only" involved.

Much of the value of KalmarSalen lies in its growing *list of customers* and in the set of *instructions* which has been developed. The list of customers is available only to the conference bureau (not to partners). KalmarSalen seeks in every case to co-ordinate all operations involving the customer, both before and after an agreement has been reached.

There are no special (boundary-transcending or in any other respect unconventional) systems for management control. Financial reporting for the arrangement as a whole has not been considered, neither has it been necessary.

Relationships among the original partners are based on a hand-shake and on trust. However, a standard contract has been prepared, and there is some tendency to use written agreements and contracts to firm up the commitments of new partners.

Ties among the joint owners are kept strong by means of "interesting meetings" and fairly frequent information. Probably the latter (when used to reinforce the impact of each success) is generally the most effective factor in holding the arrangement together.

Obviously, there is communication in the form of Christmas cards and the like. There is also some giving of certain kinds of presents. Otherwise, the system of rewards is not very well developed, although Marguerite Nilsson is currently trying to find and develop ways to reward the various stakeholders in the arrangement.

BUILDING BRIDGES BETWEEN CULTURES

Often we find that people, groups, and operations with much to offer and much to gain in a co-operative arrangement are too jealous of their respective territories to be interested. IMIT is an example of an organization with the objective of "building bridges" between the two cultures which are the foundation of Swedish industry: the culture of technology and engineers, and that of business management and financial experts.

IMIT (Institute for Management of Innovation and Technology)

IMIT's "customers" are companies and institutes of higher learning in need of developing their competence. IMIT's primary function is to pass on to them know-how in technology and leadership. The actual "service" provided by the system surrounding IMIT is thus research, studies, and a certain amount of training. The principal resources required are the researchers in the network. IMIT's contribution to the creation of value—and thus its core competence—consists in:

1. Matching important issues in industry with appropriate researchers.
2. Maintaining good relations with presumptive sources of financing.
3. Providing efficient project management.

To accomplish this mission, IMIT has established *long-term personal relationships* with key people at *leading enterprises in a number of industries*, such as Telia, Volvo, and Ericsson. These contacts generate a stream of ideas and suggestions about problems that need research. The program managers at IMIT have a role similar to that of a *movie producer*. They are to arrange financing. They are to select actors (researchers) and other personnel. They are to manage negotiations and conclude them with a contract. They are to make sure that the filming (the research) is done on time and within a budget. Finally, they are to see that the production under their responsibility reaches a large audience.

Since researchers are the critical resource, it is important for IMIT to establish long-term personal relationships with researchers at the founding institutions. For this purpose IMIT has sought to integrate its operations with those of the respective institutions and to locate its offices accordingly. Thus, despite the limited number of IMIT employees, there are offices at six locations: the Stockholm School of Economics (HHS); Chalmers Institute of Technology in Gothenburg (CTH); the Royal Institute of Technology in Stockholm (KTH); Sweden's University of Agricultural Sciences, Uppsala; the Swedish Institute of Management in Brussels (IFL); and the Lund Institute of Technology (LTH). Each of the program managers/"producers" has a regular position at one of the founding institutions.

The boundaries have been intentionally left fluid or unclear. IMIT is not to be considered as a separate institute but as closely integrated with the founding institutions: "They should feel that *they* are IMIT".

Bengt Stymne, Professor of Management at the Stockholm School of Economics, was appointed director of IMIT in 1988. Total billings were then SEK 5-6 million. Financially, results were not entirely satisfactory. Since then the actual concept of IMIT has remained unchanged; what Stymne has tried to do has been to portray it clearly and to exploit it. An important element has been the creation of the role of program manager as "producer". During Stymne's five years as director, IMIT has grown and improved its financial performance considerably. Probably IMIT now also enjoys a much more clearly established position in Swedish industry.

The critical problem has been to give IMIT an *image*, both internally and externally. The common concept must be communicated both to employees and to outside parties. There is stiff competition for the capable researchers who constitute IMIT's strategic resource. There is a definite risk that they will not devote all of their time solely to IMIT projects.

There are a number of ways in which the image is created and maintained, and the function of integration is fulfilled: a newspaper (sent out to 10,000 decision-makers in business), an information leaflet for the network, an annual meeting (for all participants in the system), meetings for each program, and a yearbook (with a brief description of current projects and of IMIT). Other means naturally used are project reporting, a common graphic design on reports, etc.

The varied affiliations of the trustees clearly serve the purpose of integration: 15 trustees represent the founding institutions, while three come from the academic world and the others are leading business executives. The same is true of the board, which consists of five leading academic figures and four influential representatives from business.

What IMIT seeks to avoid is being regarded as a parasite with little to contribute. There would then be a danger that researchers and institutions would run their projects on their own without benefiting from the opportunities for collaboration offered by IMIT. One antidote to any such tendency is an efficient operation. It is also important to have strong program managers who "own" the customer relationship and access to sources of financing for the projects. IMIT offers them and the other researchers a high fixed salary (comparable to that of a senior university lecturer). Three full-time program managers have recently been appointed professors. This success offers an opportunity to extend the network to new locations, but also poses the problem of recruiting committed program managers and "producers".

The administrative core is fragmented and dispersed, with personnel problems as a consequence. For Stymne, whose office is located elsewhere, the situation has been hard to handle.

In Stymne's vision of IMIT and its development, there are a maximum of eight program areas. For each area someone performs the role of the "producer", whose primary loyalty is to IMIT. The management group, consisting of the program managers and the director, meets regularly. International co-operation is extensive; for example, there are a number of different European projects.

6

Renovation

When a business is not doing well enough, the traditional strategic remedy is to identify strengths and weaknesses, threats and opportunities. The analysis focuses on the company and its environment: customers, competitors, etc. Management often concludes that the company needs to upgrade its own "in house" competence by hiring new employees, close down operations that cannot be saved, and so forth. In an IO perspective, all resources would be considered as the company's "own" even when it does not own them in a formal sense. They thus become potentially available for creating value for the customer. Unlike the traditional approach to business development, the IO perspective enables a company to grow without becoming larger. A traditional strategic analysis often concludes that the company needs more resources of its own if it wants to develop. Acquiring these resources takes time and costs money. In the end management may find the barrier to growth so high that the company simply abandons the whole project.

When an IO perspective is introduced into the strategic analysis, partnership becomes a preferred solution in the search for additional resources. As a result, less time is lost in reaching the market.

True, this approach exists in embryonic form when a company after a conventional strategic analysis decides to discontinue manufacturing its own components and to purchase them from outside suppliers (outsourcing). But our concept of an imaginary organization is far more dynamic: management purposefully cultivates the competence of partners and considers the establishment of long-term relationships to be in the strategic interest of the company.

In the three cases to which we will refer, the initial situation was one which should have been producing better results. The first two cases are about activating and reinforcing existing collaboration. One of the alternatives under consideration was to acquire some of the needed competence by hiring new employees, but instead management opted for a kind of exclusive supplier relationship. When we discussed this decision with management, they said that the IO perspective had helped them; in their view, it was particularly important to discover hidden patterns and to make conscious choices of appropriate ways to cultivate the network. (All case studies cited in this chapter are presented in greater detail in the Appendix.)

STOPPING A DECLINE IN PROFITS

Companies with profitability problems often respond by trying to improve their internal efficiency through layoffs, other cost-cutting measures, and the like. Similarly, when bankruptcy is threatening and creditors are knocking on the door, the normal procedure is to determine the company's worth mainly on the basis of its own balance sheet and income statement. Such an introverted and limited frame of reference blinds management to new and fruitful solutions. By passing on what we have learned from Svenska Pressbyrån and SCF, we would like to show how another frame of reference, the perspective of the imaginary organization (IO), can help us to see what is possible and what resources are actually available to the company.

Svenska Pressbyrån

Until the 1980s, Svenska Pressbyrån was managed as a chain of news-stands. There was a convenience-store operation, known as Pia Närköp, but it was small. Then came the transformation of the news-stands into convenience stores. Sales and profits rose steadily until 1990, when profits fell sharply. In 1991 there was a major loss. In 1990 the new managing director, Ulf Bergenudd, and his management team had analyzed the financial situation and the trend in demand. Both analyses indicated that Pressbyrån was headed for serious financial difficulty. The demand for tobacco products and news publications, which accounted for 50% of sales, was expected to decline—it did, by 20%. Management concluded that the downturn which they foresaw would be devastating to profitability and that the only remedy was to develop other products. The essential elements of the survival strategy were the following:

- Adding new products.
- Employee development.
- Development and adaptation of the store layout to fit the new product assortment.

The transformation process included changing the Pressbyrån image from "government-owned; surly personnel; bureaucratic; expensive; dull; over-the-counter purchase of candy, newspapers, and lottery tickets; messy" to: "an active and imaginative chain of retail stores with a strong image; with bright, clean stores and news-stands where people come primarily for impulse purchasing at attractive prices of brand-name products which provide entertainment and a sense of well-being; service by alert, pleasant, and knowledgeable employees".

The real assets on which this renovation was built were the 350,000 customers per day in 1990 and a comprehensive knowledge of customer needs and expectations. When the man in the street goes to the nearest Pressbyrån store, he is in a hurry, and often does not know what he will end up buying, except that he intends to consume it right away. The opportunity that management saw in their imagination was based partly on what they knew about the customer base, and partly on their awareness—quite natural in a trading company—of valuable assets in the form of established relationships with successful suppliers of leading brand-name products.

Examples of the expanded assortment of Pressbyrån products include popular CDs—with the pocket selection of the Top Ten or Twenty largest-selling hits—and Pressbaren (a snack bar). The common denominator is that the concept was developed by management and the products and services are supplied by carefully chosen companies. Relationships between Pressbyrån and suppliers are increasingly assuming the form of partnerships with a limited number of actors.

To illustrate how this arrangement has developed, we are adding a somewhat more detailed description of Pressbaren. The basic concept is one of *industrialized fast food* adapted to fit Svenska Pressbyrån. The other essential features are the following:

- The *delivery system*, in which Pressbyrån is responsible for refrigeration, store facilities, and personnel. Sandwiches and fruit are provided by local suppliers, juice by Brämhults, and yoghurt and other milk-based products by Margarinbolaget and the dairies. The juice and sandwiches are delivered together with the morning newspapers. Freshly brewed coffee, fruit, and salads are also part of the concept.

- *Letting the customer do some of the work*; the customer himself fills the special Pressbaren bag with the goods he wants to buy.

- *Image and credibility* by being known as a chain with a clear profile and quality.

- *Employees* who know how to serve customers. Management believes it understands the preferences of Pressbyrån's 350,000 customers a day (in 1994), and at each location the kind of books, fast food, candy, newspapers and magazines which customers expect. Customers enjoy coming into a store where they will get a laugh as well as find what they were originally looking for.

- The *customer base* of people who are buying for immediate consumption. They have seldom given much thought to what they want; what they purchase depends on what they see.

- The responsibility for the development of the *concept* is with headquarters. Management at first believed that triangular sandwiches would be a good way to create an identity. As it turned out, though, many customers asked for traditional round open sandwiches topped with beet salad and meatballs. So these items were added to the assortment. Headquarters is also responsible for the physical environment—that is, the store layout. There is a special blue cooler with a "Pressbaren" decal to be consistent with the concept and to reinforce it. Although the basic features of the concept are centrally determined, management encourages local initiatives like adding salads. The local Pressbyrån managers are also responsible for the selection and form of co-operation with local suppliers, primarily of sandwiches and salads.

• Initially management had to devote much of its time to winning an internal battle. It was important for all employees to understand and accept the concept. A concept centered on fast food was naturally new for Pressbyrån and meant a departure from the customary product assortment and delivery procedures.

Development along these new lines began in 1993 and has been in progress for a couple of years. In May 1994 there was a Pressbaren (snack bar) at 170 of the 430 locations. At the outset of 1993, 10,000 sandwiches a week were sold at SEK 25 apiece; weekly sales reached 20,000 in 1995.

Pressbaren is a good example of a new business which a tradition-bound company can develop by regarding external suppliers as resources and opportunities. Svenska Pressbyrån was thus able to grow "larger than actual size", with:

• Greater resources than shown by the balance sheet.
• More "involvees" than employees.
• Customers doing part of the work.

Other consequences of this approach have been that:

• Central administration has been reduced by 30%.

• In addition to news-stands/stores owned outright, some are owned by independent storekeepers.

• The collaboration between Svenska Pressbyrån and its suppliers has created a strong sense of identity; one purpose of the organization, which features product managers, is to develop and maintain solid relationships with suppliers.

The introduction of Pressbaren was also a way to test demand before entering into the partnership which has now been established with Blimpers. It gave Svenska Pressbyrån an opportunity to free itself still more from its former news-stand stigma, and it provided new sales which compensated for the continuing decline in press and tobacco products. As for Blimpers, collaboration gave them a stronger foothold in Sweden as well as knowledge of the market.

In 1964 Anthony Conza and some of his friends started a sand-wich shop at home in New Jersey. They offered Americans a new, healthier sandwich as an alternative to the sandwiches richer in fat which were sold in other shops all around them. To emphasize the uniqueness of the new sandwich, they gave it a name of its own—"Blimpie". Today, some 32 years later, Blimpie is the next largest chain of sandwich shops in the USA. It is represented all over the USA through its own shops and in partnership with others: convenience stores, service stations, hospitals, and schools. Just like Pressbyrån, Blimpie is there where people are.

SCF

When Marika Markland became managing director in the early 1980s, SCF (= Svenska Civilekonomföreningen; transl: the Swedish Association of School of Economics Graduates) was facing a crisis:

- The *program of continuing education* offered only a small number of courses.
- The association's *magazine, Ekonomen*, was running at an enor-mous loss, which the association could not sustain.
- A few of the *local chapters* were quite active. Some were less active. Some were not functioning at all.
- The *financial situation* was a problem that overshadowed all others. It was uncertain whether the organization could survive financially.

The cornerstone for renovating SCF was its store of knowledge which had accumulated over many years of contact with the member-ship. SCF was founded back in 1912. What it had of value was a list of members and knowledge of their professional interests and information needs.

The principal reasons for choosing an IO solution instead of building an SCF with greater resources were the following:

- There was no money to employ people with the right skills. At the same time, there were too many employees with the wrong skills. The number of employees was reduced sharply, partly to cut costs, partly to remove employees who lacked the necessary competence. With an IO solution it is easier to acquire the skills needed for each function.

- Marika Markland thought it would be fun to work with an imaginary organization.

Over a 10-year period SCF has intentionally built up an imaginary organization. The core competence which SCF provides and which makes SCF interesting to so many partners rests on:

1. The data base of customers with names, positions, companies, addresses, telephone numbers, records of participation in SCF's courses, and the subjects studied.
2. The data base of suppliers of various services, primarily in education, with names and subjects taught; the managing director also has other information on suppliers.

Both data bases are kept up-to-date. Of course the information stored is of value, but it is not the only reason why the system works. Also required is the ability to formulate relevant course themes to include in the continuing education program and in the magazine *Ekonomi & Styrning* (an appropriate English title might be "Financial and Management Control"), and to act as a talent scout in finding new people who can improve the delivery system or interesting potential in the people who are already included in the data base.

The following solutions have become established for the continuing education program:

- One project manager for each course, reporting to the managing director.
- Clear procedures for administration and mailing of correspondence to course participants and faculty both before and after the courses have been held.
- A development organization consisting of the project managers as a group or in subgroups.
- Deliberate cultivation of relationships with various independent lecturers.
- Also, close to the managing director, a number of people who contribute ideas (including an editorial advisory board for the magazine).

SCF is basically an organization in which all operations are projects staffed by non-employees. Examples include marketing campaigns, the controller function, computer development projects, and the entire day-to-day computer operation. Many of the "involvees" are independent consultants. They may also be regarded as circus performers or prima donnas with no desire to work together as a team, neither are they obliged to. The managing director, and also the other non-employees with "management responsibility" at SCF, try to cajole each of them into doing his best to create a product/service of high value to the customer. These prima donnas like being part of a faculty and have in fact shown that they can work together in groups.

Why do prima donnas work so well together in imaginary organizations? No one has a pet interest or territory to defend. Their only interest is to benefit the customer. The territories that do exist have dynamic, fluctuating boundaries. The system must have certain boundaries between participants to be interesting to the customer. And each participant must have his own particular sphere of influence.

The imaginary organization works best for Markland when she reaches an understanding with each lecturer one at a time, while creating the overall solution by herself. She has found it virtually impossible to specify the contribution of each involvee in a formal agreement. For example, there is no contract with the Editor-in-Chief of the magazine. When someone does ask for a contract, a very general one is drafted. The virtue of having no written agreements is that the managing director and the involvees talk with each other about how things are going. If there is a written contract, the parties often look first at what it says they may do. Also, the problem that many have heard but no-one has understood can only be dealt with by talking directly with each person.

How stable over the long run is an organization with such an extensive operation, so much of which is centered around the managing director, and so few permanent employees?

> Much of the operation is dependent on someone who works the way I do, but that person need not be me (says Marika Markland).

When the managing director and the two other permanent employees go home in the evening, do they "take the company with them", so that if they should not come back the next day, only an empty shell would be left of the business?

> They would not be likely to do that. Both customers and "involvees" are from the business world. Sweden is a small country, and rumors spread quickly. If someone acquired a reputation for "taking the company with him", for leaving his employer in the lurch, he would probably be considered disloyal and would have a hard time finding new work.

Does SCF have any structural capital?

> The structural capital includes the network, in which diversity provides stability. You cannot just manipulate this network at will. The people in it decide for themselves what they want to do and with whom they want to work.

Is there anything that might become a problem for SCF?

> I don't believe that the issues we have been talking about can become problems. There is a potential problem, though, and it could become a major one. If individual board members of local SCF chapters start "campaigns" from a limited point of view and devoted entirely to some special interest, without regard to the operation as a whole, serious damage could be done.

COMPETENCE GAP

Various circumstances can produce a situation in which employee competence no longer fits company requirements. A competence gap can arise, for example, when a number of skilled employees start reaching retirement age, or when the company needs to upgrade employee skills to keep pace with technological developments.

Lorentzen & Wettre

Lorentzen & Wettre supplies the world's pulp and paper companies with advanced equipment for product control and process optimization. The recession in the early 1990s undermined the company's profitability. Up to that point the company itself had manufactured most of the components it needed. When demand fell, there was not enough work for the employees. Management realized that the time had come to rethink the company's way of doing business. They decided to phase out the manufacture of components in favor of closer collaboration with partners. An additional reason for that decision was that many of those employed in component manufacture were approaching retirement; among them was the Director of Manu-facturing. The company's previous experience with outside suppliers had been quite satisfactory. Continuing to manufacture components would have called for investment in advanced equipment and in training for junior employees. Moreover, capacity utilization for the new equipment would be too low.

The company began to negotiate with outside suppliers and was offered prices below the cost of continuing to manufacture its own components. In the summer of 1992, all component production was turned over to outside suppliers, while design, assembly, and final quality control remained in the hands of the company.

The products of Lorentzen & Wettre are manufactured in series of 5–15 units. Since the company's product range is so extensive, many different kinds of components are required. For that reason, the company has to deal with some 200 component manufacturers. Annual billings from the largest of these suppliers hardly reach SEK 2 million. Most suppliers are small family businesses in the Stock-holm area. Many are run by immigrants.

The items supplied are mostly standard components, which Lorentzen & Wettre buys where the price is best. In the case of components which the company itself has developed, there is particularly close collaboration with some ten suppliers; their relationship with Lorentzen & Wettre is essentially the same as if they were its employees. The dialogue is similar to the one between the boss and the people under him. Suppliers frequently visit the company, usually to speak with employees in the assembly and inventory-control departments.

These contacts give the suppliers a sense of involvement and enhance the exchange of information on how partners are doing financially and otherwise. Since a major portion of supplier capacity is dedicated to filling the requirements of Lorentzen & Wettre, a supplier without enough orders from the company will face serious financial problems. While management has no other, more system-atic, way of collecting information on the current situation of these partners, Lorentzen & Wettre's network of contacts is so extensive that alternative suppliers can be found at short notice.

How has the work of the management team been affected by the change? The clearest difference is that more attention is now paid to inventory control, which occupies a prominent place on the agenda, and inventories have been reduced. By contrast, time formerly spent on the manufacturing department can now be devoted to other matters.

7
Extension

Fortunately, companies seldom find themselves in crises that must be resolved by renovation. Successive extensions usually suffice to make the company competitive again. To give its business new strength usually requires more of a company than just finding additional customers for what it is already doing. More likely, it may have to seek new ways of interfacing with the customer—imaginatively contributing to the creation of new value after discovering the value, old or new, in its own resources and in those of existing and potential partners.

In traditional strategic analysis we may refer to new businesses in the bud, although perhaps only after thorough groundwork in the form of studies and development efforts. This possibility naturally exists in an imaginary organization, but the approach is different. When we take stock of our resources we should include those of our partners. We may also find it appropriate to acquire a new partner. The literature describes various forms of strategic alliances in development projects, primarily in high-technology fields. We want to show how even very simple linkages of this kind may be beneficial and why we need an IO perspective to see them and to understand how to deal with them.

In several of our six cases under this heading, new linkages and sometimes new partners were required. However, we have not classified these cases as examples of renovation, since they are primarily about increasing sales of products similar to existing ones, or using new technology to upgrade the operation and offer a more highly developed version of the former product. In discussing how to accomplish such an objective, we have been able to convince our interviewees that an IO perspective can provide a clearer picture of the appropriate pattern and course of action to assure continued success. Some case studies are presented in greater detail in the Appendix, as indicated in the text.

CHRONIC SHORTAGE OF FINANCING

The Värmdö Municipal Office of Cultural Affairs

Värmdö is a semirural community east of Stockholm. It is a separate "kommun", or municipality, with its own Office of Cultural Affairs (Värmdö kommuns kultursekretariat) (see also Appendix). At the Office people have realized that if they take a different approach to their work more can be accomplished with the subsidies granted to associations. They can help these associations to create more for their money, and along lines consistent with the cultural ambitions of the municipality.

A good example is the program of artistic activities in the schools. Here the Office attempts to involve the schools in exposing students to the arts in various forms. At first the schools and their cultural officials were very cautious. Today they believe that they offer good programs and that the credit is theirs rather than that of the Office. This outcome resulted from the strategy deliberately adopted by the Office, which did most of the work. To win the support of the schools, the Office helped them to create value by giving them a sense of participation and of achieving success through their own efforts. Today officials responsible for the arts at their schools want to know about a number of activities, share their experience, and find new ideas through the joint council set up by the Office, which also serves as the hub of the council.

The program of cultural activities in the schools was a response to impulses from a variety of sources, and was also a result of the creativity of the Office and of its strong desire to gain a foothold in the schools. The people at the Office have had to be both perceptive and persistent. The Office has also succeeded in persuading associations and educational federations active in similar areas to work together and to establish joint projects for mutual support and exchange of experience. In this way the parties involved can obtain more for their money, and the additional value created furthers the cultural ambitions of the municipality. Examples include a local historic-preservation council and a council for the cultural environment.

Contacts and co-operation have been furthered by an exchange of annual reports. Also, a degree of formal control is exercised by the Office by means of subsidy guidelines which it has prepared and follows in practice. In the voluntary councils (such as the local historic-preservation council), statements of common objectives are drafted and later reviewed through joint meetings, visits, and some exchange of statistics.

Each year the Office gives a very popular "staff party" for all contacts and enthusiasts—the annual St. Lucia Coffee Party shortly before Christmas.

The Office enables the various parts of the "spider web" to create added value through

- Its extensive knowledge of various cultural activities.
- A large network in the municipality which includes all the different associations, local politicians, and the various parties with a commercial interest in cultural activities.
- A large network which includes government authorities in the cultural area, writers, theater groups, artists, etc.
- A network of contacts for various kinds of project subsidies.
- Allocation of subsidies.
- An exhibition hall in the library for use by associations.
- A news bulletin and a catalog of cultural events.

The Office allocates subsidies and funnels various kinds of grants to some of the associations and educational federations in the spider web, as part of its own function as the spider. However, the principal assets of the Office are its professional knowledge and network of contacts. These are the assets which are most utilized and most appreciated by associations, educational federations, and other parties in the cultural sphere.

The Office exercises its leadership differently in different parts of the spider web. For example, when the programs of artistic activities were first established at the schools, the focus was largely on developing appropriate forms of co-operation. Once the programs were in place, the emphasis shifted to being open to innovation and creating new expectations to avoid stagnation. The Office does not interfere in the efforts by the schools to realize common objectives.

At the Office people have learned to work through others and without regard to their own prestige (the associations are free to take the credit for any success achieved), to be perceptive, and to avoid being bureaucratic.

SUBMITTING THE WINNING BID

To win a contract to manufacture a new product, or at a volume far exceeding normal levels, a company must mobilize all its resources and capacity to think along new lines. The realization that the existing range of goods or services only partly fits the specifications can be overwhelming, particularly if the competitors are major corporations which to a large extent already supply the products/services called for. One response is to assume the role of leader enterprise in forming an "*ad hoc* syndicate", linking together the resources and competence of several partner companies.

SATT Control

SATT Control (SC) is an electronics company in the Alfa Laval group. SC sells electronic products and control systems to various industries and customer categories: food products, municipalities, warehouses, industrial ventilation, etc. It has 550 employees in Sweden, and about the same number abroad.

How can SC bid against ABB, Siemens, and other large corporations on major contracts for equipment which the company has never sold before? SC does so by acting as *system integrator*. In this role SC co-ordinates the contracting syndicate by preparing the system description and dividing the system into various subsystems; each potential partner thus bids on the contract for a part of the total system. Describing the system and dividing it into subsystems are two elements of core competence. What is required is the capacity to specify reliability standards, to classify them according to different reliability categories, and to design solutions to various reliability problems. The know-how to perform mean-time-between-failure

(MTBF) analyses is critical. What makes a company competitive in this area is its ability to design a system architecture in which system functions are placed at the right level so as to reduce complexity and take advantage of modern information technology. Innovations in system architecture make it possible to transfer functions from one subsystem to another, often by decentralization, which in turn opens up new possibilities.

As "integrator", the company is familiar with the overall system. The breakdown into subsystems is facilitated by standard procedures for transmission of information. A critical factor is the capacity to calculate volumes of information. Without its know-how, acquired from other operations, in systems configuration and partition into subsystems, the company would not have been equal to this role.

A collaboration agreement governing the distribution of risks is reached with the other participants in the project. Here SC draws on the competence it has acquired from all its previous projects. Normally risks are distributed among partners in proportion to their respective share of the total amount of the bid. In other words, skill in drafting contracts is important. The contract among the partners often includes clauses on confidentiality in regard to the customer, liability for damages, etc.

Fundamental to the collaboration among partners in this kind of project, in which each is dependent on the other, is the notion that "what is good for you is good for me". Often co-operation is better between companies than between different departments of the same company or different companies in the same corporate group. Familiarity with networks and with other potential partners is important. SC often purchases "standardized" services, such as assembly; it is easy to specify what is required without having it performed by the company's own employees. Thus, the problem of *finding work for the company's own resources* is avoided.

Project management is important as a resource and as an element of SC's competence. After the company has received an order for a project, one of the first actions taken is to prepare a clear specification of functions *together with the customer*. This process is fundamental—and time-consuming. The initial step is to specify what the system is supposed to do, before deciding how it is to be done—that is, designing the system architecture. The specifications should be correct from the outset; if they are not, the error will reappear all down the line. It is also important that all partners agree on the basic concept of the project.

SC has a reason for devoting so much effort to preparing bids on major contracts; by bidding the company makes itself known to potential customers. "People will have you in mind"; they will come back with other inquiries, which may provide opportunities to sell smaller systems and projects. SC's reputation will spread throughout the customer's organization.

Sales director Rolf Pettersson asked himself two questions: "What is our core competence?"; and "What functions and resources should we have under our own roof?" He continued, "We must be careful not to end up as a run-of-the-mill consulting firm".

Perhaps the critical factor is the company's know-how in the production and design of certain key parts of the system. It may also be important to have a number of unique components or software systems, such as systems for graphic presentation.

INCREASE MARKET SHARE WITH THE EXISTING CUSTOMER BASE

How a company handles its customer base directly affects both short-run and long-run profitability. Customer turnover is a major factor in this regard. It has been calculated that for certain companies in service industries reducing the number of customers lost by 5% would result in a profitability increase of 25–85%, depending on the industry. A company which has been losing 15–20% of its customers each year can more than double its growth if it cuts the rate of customer loss in half.

In the experience of most companies, business done with existing customers is normally much more profitable than with new customers, if the cost of developing the latter is taken into consideration. Therefore, increasing market share among existing customers is important for maintaining and improving profitability.

Alfa Laval Agri Manure Business

Alfa Laval Agri Manure Business is an example of a company which plans to strengthen its position with customers by collaborating with partners. The business operates in Western Europe and

North America. Annual sales were SEK 200 million in 1994, and the goal for 1996 is SEK 600 million.

To grow in a market where the number of customers is declining (farmers), Alfa Laval has identified manure-handling equipment as a potential growth area. The farmer needs equipment at every link of the following value chain: manure removal/transportation/pumping/storage/mixing/treatment/test sampling/spreading.

Through Odin, a wholly owned subsidiary, the company today enjoys a strong position on the Scandinavian market. However, the product line is too narrow, and management is looking for partners to expand sales, primarily in Europe. The aim is to benefit from the special products and competence of different partners, while offering them greater sales volume through Alfa Laval Agri's marketing companies. The arrangement may involve a total of five or six partners, each of which concentrates on its home market, with some exports in addition. The organization is primarily production-oriented.

According to the concept, each partner is to possess its own specific competence in:

- Product development.
- Production.
- Providing market service.

Alfa Laval Agri seeks exclusive agreements for marketing the products of its partners through its own marketing organization under the Alfa Laval Agri brand.

A number of important issues must be resolved if the company's strategy with respect to its partners is to be successful:

- How to co-ordinate the network of partners to achieve the desired volume benefits in production, purchasing, and R&D?
- How to respond quickly to changes in market conditions?
- How to co-ordinate the product line to avoid duplication of product development by different companies?
- How dependent should/must partners be on Alfa Laval Agri? How to reduce their sensitivity to changes in volume?

- How to create healthy internal competition, while avoiding war, among the various partners?

- How to create a system of quality control which guarantees high quality and continued confidence in the Alfa Laval Agri brand name?

- How to establish methods for investment calculations which will produce comparable figures for total product costs?

- How to obtain royalties and license income to finance the product center?

The establishment of a product center is being considered as an answer to these questions. The center would include the following functions:

- Engineering development (co-ordination but not central product development).
- Methods for product development and its support.
- Product co-ordination.
- Development of the product line.
- Product documentation.

The product center is intended to provide regular sales follow-up and quality statistics for each product code and partner. In addition, the product center should have the competence to provide support in:

- Total quality management.
- Information technology.
- Logistics/distribution.
- Productivity growth/continued improvement.

The flow of orders should go directly from the marketing companies to production. This procedure calls for thorough product documentation and well-defined product structures and article numbers.

Regular meetings are held with the partners for the purpose of:

- Exchanging observations based on experience.
- Providing an overall view of how the business is doing.
- Creating a sense of joint endeavor among partners.

- Changing the product assortment and promoting common use of the same components.

ENLARGING THE CUSTOMER BASE

In the new logic of value creation, it is unclear in some situations who is the customer and who stands to gain from what. Such a situation arises when several companies share the same customer base and work together, in a manner benefiting all parties, for the purpose of offering the customer something of value.

Lord's

One example of an enlarged customer base is found in the collaboration between Lord's and American Express. What could a company in Stockholm, with two or three employees and selling made-to-order men's clothing, possibly have in common with a company in the credit-card business? Nothing, except that both parties benefit from co-operating: American Express offers its cardholders a discount on made-to-order men's clothing at Lord's, if they pay with their American Express card. Through this co-operative arrangement, Lord's can substantially enlarge its customer base; increased sales make up for the revenue lost on the discount.

For American Express, the collaboration with Lord's is a way to compete on the payments market. Lord's can establish relationships with new customers in exchange for a discount. By paying with their American Express cards, customers can buy made-to-order clothing at a reduced price. But Lord's has no tailor of its own. The suits are made in Germany and the shirts in Hong Kong.

A NEW COMPETITIVE SITUATION

Changing market conditions encourage and nourish the process of business development. The changes may relate to the preferences and behavior of customers, suppliers, and competitors, as well as factors affecting the general economic climate, such as business cycles, exchange rates, inflation, and interest rates. Legislation and government regulations can also involve major changes for companies forced to comply.

The Stockholm Stock Exchange

The Stockholm Stock Exchange (Stockholms Fondbörs) (see also Appendix) is an example of an operation which has undergone substantial change since the mid-1980s. A number of factors were pushing the Swedish stock market to innovate: growing awareness of the importance of low transaction costs; parliamentary decisions to deregulate stock trading in a number of countries; a shift of trading from countries like Germany, France, The Netherlands, and Sweden to the London Stock Exchange; and the ensuing internalization of the market.

Before becoming President of the Stockholm Stock Exchange in the mid-1980s, Bengt Rydén had been director of SNS (the Swedish Industrial Council for Social and Economic Studies). Brought in on the wave of change which was sweeping over the stock markets of the world, subjecting all stock exchanges to basically the same kind of pressure to adapt, Bengt Rydén had the advantage of not being bound by the traditional stock-market way of thinking.

As a newcomer to the industry, Bengt Rydén devoted much of his time to analyzing the environmental forces which might affect the industry. His conclusion was that stock-market trading was too expensive. Transaction costs were accepted out of convention and custom. The stock exchange which offered lower transaction costs would gain market share. The technical solution to the cost problem was already known: modern information technology (IT). At this point neither the Stockholm Stock Exchange Council nor the Department of Finance nor the Swedish Finance Commission were very aware of the necessity to reform trading on the Exchange. The need was identified by Exchange management, which responded by designing an imaginary organization (IO). This IO provided a solution for "going electronic", given the fact that the Exchange had no IT competence of its own. Both software and hardware were developed in co-operation with external suppliers. A few other stock exchanges which had begun to use IT served as examples for study.

Once the groundwork had been done, the Stock Exchange Council decided in 1986 to invest in an IT solution; procurement followed in 1987, and the system was put in service in 1989. In Europe trading was done mostly on the floor of the stock exchanges. The

Swedish brokers wanted to continue with floor trading and saw no value or personal advantage in an IT solution. Moreover, many of them feared—and rightly so—that IT would affect their working conditions and far from all of them could make the necessary adjustment. Nevertheless, resistance to IT was not especially strong or well organized, probably because of the traditional Swedish openness to technical improvements. The opposition in other countries proved considerably more stubborn.

By its decision the Stock Exchange Council acted before the belief that stock trading would be internationalized became generally accepted. The decision by the British parliament to deregulate trading on the Exchange (called the Big Bang of October, 1986, even though there was a plan for implementing the change over several years) set powerful forces in motion. Major international banks gained the right to own British brokerage firms and were then able to trade in the securities of other countries. Once the banks had become actors on the London Stock Exchange in 1987, management at other stock exchanges throughout Europe looked on as an ever-growing share of the trading shifted to London. Internationalization was no longer a possibility; it was a fact.

The first step in this direction for Swedish stock trading was the acceptance of the belief that IT would be introduced and become strategically important as a means of competition. This belief opened the way for the IT decision. Actually, the decision could have been postponed for a few years; in Switzerland an IT solution was not adopted until 1995.

Assumptions and guesses about the pace of deregulation and the internationalization of stock trading determined the timing of the IT decision: 1986. Particularly important was the assumption as to when the Swedish exchange controls would be abolished. When this event took place in 1989, the map of the Swedish financial world had to be redrawn.

Legal changes in the organization favored the investment in IT

An even more radical transformation, in the view of the Exchange President, was incorporation; i.e. the Exchange became a Swedish limited-liability corporation (aktiebolag). In the case of IT, outside expertise was available, and there were other stock exchanges from which to learn. Stock trading is tradition-bound. For the preceding 200 years, it had been done under the same basic legal structure. The Swedish experience with brokerage in stock options and futures shows that it is possible to operate a stock exchange with a different legal structure, that of a corporation. The radical change was that under previous law the fees charged by the Stockholm Stock Exchange could only cover costs. The reason to operate the Exchange as a corporation, and also the ambition of management, was to build up equity for security and to finance investments. Another form of legal organization, the *ekonomisk förening*, was also considered, but was rejected on the ground that it was less suitable for accumulating capital. Furthermore, it was believed that a corporation would be superior to an economic association at providing incentives for efficient financial management.

As a first step toward getting all parties used to the idea of an operation run for profit and subject to competition, a special business unit was set up at the Stock Exchange in 1987; its concept of business was to distribute information on buy and sell quotations, volume of trading, and other data needed by the actors on the Exchange. The primary purpose, in the view of management, was to introduce a different way of thinking. Management correctly anticipated the risk of conflict between the traditional monopoly culture of the Stock Exchange and the new commercial culture. Self-interest prevailed, however, once the Exchange had become familiar with the nature of a commercial operation on a limited scale. Gradually more and more people began to ask—at first mostly in jest—"Why not commercialize all stock trading, the whole thing?"

After discussions, studies, and the report of the Swedish Committee on Securities, a new stock-exchange law was proposed in 1992. The proposal included the abolition of the stock-exchange monopoly. At its own request, the Stockholm Stock Exchange would be operated as a corporation to meet the new competitive situation. The radical difference was that now shareholders would be making demands, and there would be a new model for management control emphasizing return on capital, so that the necessary funds would be available for future investments, primarily in IT.

In summary: the first step in the renovation of the Stockholm Stock Exchange was to modernize technology so as to reduce transaction costs and offer intermediaries and customers the possibility of following the market on real time; all information about a particular security would be available from a central computer. The second step was to change the legal form of organization to that of a corporation so that the Exchange could continue to finance its investments and improve its efficiency.

The flexibility which smallness allows has become a strength of the Stockholm Stock Exchange. The legal barriers to entry are gone, and technology has eliminated the distance factor. Brokers can be located in a remote country and still operate on the Swedish exchange. For Bengt Rydén, the work of renewal has exacted a heavy commitment, and it has forced him to focus on strategic issues in Sweden and internationally. Rydén proved equal to the task by being able to delegate the management of day-to-day operations and by upgrading the competence of the people who worked for him.

The Stockholm Stock Exchange has become an imaginary organization to an extreme degree, not only in the sense of active collaboration with providers of outside resources, but also in that the IT solution chosen has made the operation highly abstract. An anonymous market of buyers and sellers agree on quantities and prices over computer screens. With so many actors, none of them can dominate the market. Securities as a physical phenomenon are a thing of the past; now they are characters in a data base.

The financial results have been very promising, as is the outlook for the next few years. The future presents two principal risks: one is the threat of increasing competition from privately owned IT systems; the other is a loss of trust by the general public. A high degree of trust is important, since the Stock Exchange fulfills a number of important public functions. Therefore, the need for responsible ownership is clear. The new stock-exchange law has no provisions on ownership, and the shares of the Stockholm Stock Exchange are freely transferable. Concentration of ownership could lead to abuse, thus undermining vital public trust.

NEW TECHNOLOGY

A change in technology is a powerful driving force. Countless business-development projects, in widely differing areas, have followed in the wake of such technological innovations as the switch from electromechanics to electronics, the introduction of semi-conductors, and the use of refrigeration.

CE Fritzes

CE Fritzes (see also Appendix) is a publishing enterprise which specializes in issuing information on legal norms set by the national government (laws and regulations). Normative information of this kind has long been communicated on paper in the form of books and documents. The CD-ROM technology was developed in the 1980s as a new way to transmit information. Management was aware of the potential of the new technology and its future strategic importance. They also realized that the company lacked competence in the area. In 1990 they were facing the choice of either first starting their own in-house program to develop the necessary competence in CD-ROM before attempting to commercialize the new technology, *or* proceeding directly to commercial development and obtaining the necessary competence from outside.

Management chose the latter course, mainly because it would take less time. Commercial introduction at an early date was considered important. The required competence would be built up during the course of the project as the outside specialists involved in it passed their know-how on to the company.

For a publishing enterprise to choose an IO solution would appear normal. It would be no wild guess to assume that running a company most of whose business was publishing would be a question of "management in imaginary organizations". But not always.

CE Fritzes—like most publishers—takes a rather passive stance toward writers. Government materials are published on the terms set by the issuing authority; with the Swedish Government Publishing House (Allmänna Förlaget) as a speaking partner. In the case of Norstedts Legal Publications (Norstedts Juridik), the author submits the manuscript for printing, binding, and distribution to readers. It is fairly uncommon for the editor to make major revisions or comment on the content. Basically, the book will be published when the author has finished the manuscript. This statement applies to the traditional publishing industry. The writers need the publisher to reach the readers; the publisher does not need to call on the writers, since it has established relationships with customers who need easy access to specific information.

The first commercial application was to record *Sveriges Rikes Lag* (transl: the Law of the Realm of Sweden, a compilation of the principal Swedish codes and other statutes) on CD-ROM. No one questioned the project, which was entirely consistent with the concept of CE Fritzes' business, or the need to bring in outside expertise to staff the project, since all realized that no one in the company knew much about the new technology.

The project was launched in 1991 and completed in 1993. It was staffed as follows. In all 45 people were involved more or less actively in the project. Of these, 80% were outsiders and 20% were from the company. Those from the company worked primarily in project management, editing, and market analysis/marketing. The outsiders supplied expertise in the design of the technical systems environment and the creation of a uniform graphic presentation, CD-ROM production, registration of text, and proof-reading. The total investment in the project was SEK 7 million.

Project management could be characterized as follows:

* An enthusiastic project manager.
* A project manager who gave clear instructions.
* More was demanded of the outsiders than of the company's own employees.
* Schedules were sacred. Insistence on meeting deadlines.
* The project manager co-ordinated the various participating actors, each of whom worked in isolation from the others— "islands in a common archipelago".
* The actors were treated strictly but fairly.
* Close project follow-up.
* The outside actors regarded the project as an important future reference and as a part of their own professional development.

The core competence and critical factors possessed by CE Fritzes were the following:

* Fritzes had been issuing *Sveriges Rikes Lag* and all included texts for many years.

- Familiarity with the subject matter and a tradition of publishing works on legal subjects. Contacts with legal experts, such as justices of the Swedish Supreme Court, who had structured and checked the material.
- Proprietary rights to the title *Sveriges Rikes Lag*.
- A customer base.

After the conclusion of the project, the imaginary structure was changed; a couple of the specialists who had been involved joined CE Fritzes as employees; the continuing registration of new material was turned over to personnel on loan from a secretarial service; a telemarketing company was retained to solicit each customer group by telephone.

One difficult question is how to share profits and risks in a manner which all parties find equitable and in their own interest. A traditional solution was used in the project; the compensation of parties brought in from outside was set in negotiations on a case-to-case basis.

The development of an overall strategy

CE Fritzes is part of the Liber group, which in turn is owned by Wolters Kluwer (WK). WK is an example of a publishing enterprise oriented toward its base of customers (subscribers to *regular information* in a particular field) and their needs. To meet delivery commitments, WK has developed an infrastructure, the principal elements of which are contacts and familiarity with writers (sources), and a system of production and distribution. Taken together, these elements constitute a complete information system.

An important part of CE Fritzes' strategy is to set up a similar operation for normative information, based to a considerable degree on an imaginary organization. The critical question is how to change a culture shaped by many years of traditional publishing so that it will accept the management philosophy necessary to succeed with the new strategy, while at the same time continuing its traditional operations.

Part of the solution is to reduce the number of employees and thus make it necessary to collaborate with outside suppliers. In accordance with this policy, 17 persons were retired in 1993 under the terms of their collective employment agreement; four others resigned. No new employees will be hired.

Both in the company and in the corporate group to which it belongs, there are a number of forces working to keep CE Fritzes from becoming part of an imaginary organization.

1. The union insists on the principle that employees who have been laid off be given priority in filling any new positions created.

2. The Liber group is required by Wolters Kluwer to produce a certain overall profit; surpluses in one group company may be used to offset deficits in another. As a consequence, companies with low profitability are protected, and unprofitable businesses are allowed to continue operating. The stimulus of a minimum profit requirement at the corporate level can work like valium at the subsidiary level.

3. Since CE Fritzes is presently doing well financially, there are no unfavorable key ratios putting pressure on the company to change.

4. The word "competitor" is never mentioned, an indication that awareness of what is happening in the business environment is limited.

5. The traditional practice of publishing books and distributing them to customers has never required the company to know much about its customers. Acquiring this knowledge is a threshold which at least some parts of the company have to cross before they can work in the new way.

In a situation like this one, what strategies are available to a managing director who believes that success can be achieved by working actively in an imaginary organization?

1. Establish a subsidiary, build it up, and manage it as as if it were part of an imaginary organization. Has not been tried.

2. Establish a "garage company", with competent employees who are younger than 30 and who work at a location separate from ordinary operations. Has not been tried.

3. Start a project based on a technology with which the staff is unfamiliar. An example is the recently concluded project of recording *Sveriges Rikes Lag* on CD-ROM.

Developments 1994–1996

Under the ownership of Wolters Kluwer, operations were focused more clearly on the core business, and stiffer requirements for volume and return on investment were imposed. These changes made it necessary to improve control of production flow, customer analysis, and selling. It gradually became evident that the company was involved in two businesses so different that they would best develop as independent units: on the one hand, there was Allmänna Förlaget (the Swedish Government Publishing House), which publishes official documents; on the other, Norstedts Juridik, Aktuell Juridik, and Publica. Consequently, in 1995 CE Fritzes was split into two companies. One consisted of CE Fritzes together with Allmänna Förlaget and Fritzes InformationsCenter; the other, of Norstedts Juridik AB and the remaining operations.

The project of recording *Sveriges Rikes Lag* on CD-ROM, which we have previously described, was developed in those parts of the organization which subsequently formed Norstedts Juridik AB. The growth of Norstedts Juridik AB has followed business policies highly consistent with a principle fundamental to the perspective of the imaginary organization: the focus on the core business. We thus find a clear distinction between those functions retained entirely by the leader enterprise and those to be performed together with partners. The core business of Norstedts Juridik AB has been developed through massive investments in comprehensive data bases which include statutes, court decisions, annotations, etc. With these data bases as a foundation, new electronic products were developed in 1995 and 1996.

Organizationally, a special department, Digital Service, is responsible for the content of the data bases (GSML-format) and for assuring that these are up-to-date, etc. This department, which possesses the expertise to procure what is required for its operations, includes a director, three project managers, an engineer, and a legal adviser. The editorial staffs are responsible for applications: that is, the specification, development, and marketing of products and services. The physical work of recording material in data bases, the production of CD-ROM disks, etc., is performed by three partners. Though differing in primary focus, each of these partners can do the work of the others if necessary.

For the partner responsible for production, the co-operation and support of Norstedts Juridik AB have enabled that partner to gain competence in a previously unfamiliar area. As this partner learns and invests in new production technology, it achieves a new leading competence in the production of electronic media and offers it to Norstedts Juridik AB as well as to other customers. The development of this competence thus provides new business opportunities for both companies.

8
Observations from the Case Studies

In our case studies, the customer base is an important resource for joint use by the partners in an imaginary organization (IO). Customer relationships must be cultivated and developed with great care. Information technology often plays a significant part in holding the structure together, in making it possible to learn about meeting customer needs, and in serving as a basis for an efficient delivery system.

In the short run, it is true that the party who "owns" the relationship with the ultimate customer also commands a position of strength by having the primary right to define what creates value in the interface with the customer. But beware: customer loyalty should not be overestimated! Customers are always on the lookout for what is in their best interests and will make their choices accordingly. For that reason, the party most active in adapting to change will in time assume a leading role in the system. Innovative capacity is a critical competitive factor and will largely determine which of the competing IOs will win out in the battle for the customer. This point is illustrated by one of the case studies which we have not yet presented: Scandinavian PC Systems (SPCS) (see also Appendix).

SPCS has no employees who are good at product development. Instead, the company works with programmers, teachers, consultants, and researchers at universities and colleges in creating and developing computer programs. The role of SPCS in the system is to produce "a letter of understanding" concerning the products to be developed, to keep the relationship dynamic, and to motivate the other parties to devote their full effort to the work of development (one incentive being to offer a royalty on sales).

It is of critical importance to:

- Look for the mechanisms which produce innovation.
- Look for the place where innovative capability can be found.
- Own the customer relationship, an advantage in the short run, although no guarantee in the long run.

IMAGINATION AND CO-ORDINATION

An imaginary organization is not a perpetual-motion machine. It will neither come into existence nor grow further on its own! If anything is to happen, the first requirement is that there be an "imaginator" (see Chapter 1) who can see possibilities. While the companies in the case studies had conducted formal strategic analyses, the essential ideas emerged from informal talks which went on over a longer period of time. Intuition and a sense of potential business opportunities played a significant part in these discussions. The second requirement is that the leader enterprise assume the role of co-ordinator for the operations performed in the IO.

In our case studies we have found that the driving forces listed below have had a major dynamic effect. They appear to be general in nature and thus applicable whether the case is one of creation, renovation, or extension. The leader enterprise should:

- Be the integrator.
- View its role as that of talent scout.
- Arrange value constellations.
- Use information technology.
- Establish a jointly-owned product center.
- Create a joint council or project for the system.
- Go where it really wants to.
- Stimulate local initiative consistent with a concept of the operation as a whole.
- Cultivate co-operation that will lead to growth.

Being the integrator

Liber–Hermods (see also Chapter 1) is the integrator that enables local governments to keep control of their finances while still maintaining their local identity. Collaboration with Hermods has proved to be a viable alternative to sending secondary-school students to a neighboring municipality for a constantly mounting fee. The local school has teachers and classrooms, prepares schedules, etc. Hermods provides the textbooks, arranges introductory days and continuing education for teachers, and holds examinations. Hermods very deliberately cultivates relationships with teachers and authors of textbooks. Teachers are given further training and must never be given cause for dissatisfaction with the teaching materials provided.

Being a talent scout

The key is the ability to "read" what the actors in the network like to do and are capable of doing, and to conduct a dialog with them to create and evaluate intriguing ideas: to recognize talent and to give it a challenge!

One example is SCF (see also Chapter 6 and Appendix), which follows this approach to developing its program of continuing education. The Managing Director "reads" what people in the network can and want to do, and makes a financial assessment of the market potential for new courses in which their talent would provide the essential ingredient. This method works best when the Managing Director can reach separate agreements, one at a time, on what each party is to provide, and then—without involving outsiders—put together the total package. Many of the people in the SCF base of resources and competence are independent consultants, whom the Managing Director considers "prima donnas" unwilling to adapt to others. The Managing Director looks for the best of what each has to offer and joins these parts together in a service of high value to the customer.

Innovation by being a talent scout calls for an ability to learn in detail the strengths, weaknesses and desires of talented people, and then to weigh all these factors in preparing services/products of high value in the interface with the customer.

Arranging value constellations

KalmarSalen (see also Chapter 5 and Appendix) is the hub of a growing visitor and tourist industry in Kalmar, a small coastal city in south-eastern Sweden. The components are:

- The concert hall.
- Hotel rooms in the city.
- The congress and conference business.
- Meals.
- Transportation.
- Participant administration.

The business derives its market power from the way it is run. A small staff of permanent employees is charged with administration. For congresses/conferences KalmarSalen provides a complete conference package which includes meeting halls, hotel rooms, meals, transportation, participant administration, and other related arrangements. The core competence consists of two essential elements, both of which are controlled by the leader enterprise: the conference bureau, which is important for "owning" the contact with the customer, and the co-ordinator; one of the four permanent staff employees is responsible for contract administration, prepares manuals, and provides all co-ordination. The essential skill is to see which services will provide value for each particular organizer (customer) and to arrange the value constellation of suppliers most appropriate in each case.

Using information technology

Information is becoming a strategic resource in business. Attending to this resource and using it profitably can be critical for success.

For the Stockholm Stock Exchange (see also Chapter 7 and Appendix), the investments of recent years in a computerized system for efficient stock trading proved decisive. There are other examples in convenience goods; producers, wholesalers, and retailers exchange information on sales and orders using a combination of computer and telecommunication technologies.

Establishing a jointly-owned product center

One strategy for growth on a market with fewer and fewer customers is to select a small corner of it, or niche, and then add what is necessary by actively collaborating with partners. Alfa Laval Agri Manure Business (see also Chapter 7) is an example. Their problem has been a shrinking customer base, since the number of farmers is continually diminishing. Their strategy has been to identify manure handling as a potential growth area and to broaden the product range by establishing relationships with partners. Through collaboration Alfa Laval Agri can add special products and gain access to expertise in product development, production, and market service. Partners enjoy increased sales through Alfa Laval Agri's marketing subsidiaries. The result is greater value for the customer, not only in direct customer benefit, but also for Alfa Laval Agri, which can make better use of the potential in its customer capital.

To co-ordinate the network of partners, the company is considering the establishment of a "jointly owned" product center. Co-ordination would cover a number of areas: engineering development, development efforts and improvement of competence in general, products, development of the product assortment, and product documentation. The product center would be a meeting ground for the partners in the system, for sharing experience, for providing an overview of what is happening in the industry, for creating a team spirit among the partners, and for discussions about what else they might do together.

The core competence which Alfa Laval Agri protects and cultivates is its expertise in the physiology and biology of both animals and human beings who spend time in barns and stables, and also in assembling components into products for so-called aggressive environments.

Creating a joint council or project for the system

The essence of the business of an IO resides in the system itself rather than with any of the individual parties. Therefore, it may be appropriate to make a joint council or project the arena of innovation. An example is the arrangement for promoting cultural activities in the Stockholm suburb of Värmdö. One of the efforts of the

Värmdö Municipal Office of Cultural Affairs (see also Chapter 7 and Appendix) has been at involving the schools in introducing the arts to children. A deliberate strategy of the Office has been to support school officials responsible for the arts, to give them a sense of participation, to let them take the credit for any success achieved—all the while doing most of the work. Today these school officials are curious about a wealth of different activities, they share their experience, and they bring up new ideas in the joint council which was created at the initiative of the Office.

The Office is also succeeding in its efforts to promote co-operation between associations and educational federations in the form of joint projects for mutual support and for sharing experience. The result has been development and innovation in the cultural sphere.

Going where the leader enterprise really wants to

It is a cultural tradition in conventional companies to begin any discussion on innovation by referring to existing resources. In this respect an IO enterprise is quite different; it sees the whole world as its resource.

Folkoperan (see also Chapter 5 and Appendix) is an exciting example. It was founded in Stockholm in 1976 as an independent touring theater ensemble by a newly graduated conductor, a movie director who worked mostly with film advertisements, and a business manager with singing ambitions. What they all wanted was to work with opera, and that common desire led their way. Reinforced by a written statement of artistic and "business" objectives, Folkoperan has developed into its present-day operation.

Stimulating local initiative consistent with a concept of the operation as a whole

A solid sense of identity allows for an understanding of the operation as a whole, while also furnishing the confidence to permit and stimulate local initiative. At Svenska Pressbyrån (see also Chapter 6 and Appendix) (which before renovation was just a nationwide chain of news-stands), the identity of the whole lies in the image of the enterprise in combination with brand names owned by powerful suppliers.

Local initiative is stimulated by the dialog between management and the employees of the local Pressbyrån stores.

"Management by learning" is the basis of the management philosophy. Some of the essential elements are the concept of the operation as a whole, open boundaries, independence, knowledge of local conditions, and the requirement that the managing director, through a process of dialog, sees that all personnel understand these elements.

An example of local initiative consistent with a concept of the whole is the decision by Pressbyrån to sell fast food for "people on the go" under the name "Pressbaren". This concept is based on:

- A *delivery system* in close co-operation with suppliers.
- *Letting the customer do some of the work.*
- Headquarters responsibility for the *concept* and its development.

CONCLUSIONS

The case studies presented illustrate the following:

- It is possible to develop a growing business without becoming any larger.
- A concept of business should specify "what for whom". In fact, concepts of business are often expressed in this manner. A description which also includes "the way in which products/services are developed, produced, and distributed" limits the thinking of the company; depending on the wording, it may even make it impossible to develop an IO perspective.
- Development through active co-operation without being cheated is possible when each party controls, cultivates, and can defend its core competence.
- It is important to win the internal struggle. It is natural for the company's own employees to want to be involved in development without giving much thought to whether they are the most competent to do so. To reduce staff is one way to prepare the company for the imaginary organization. Another driving force is present when the company is under heavy pressure to change from the business environment. A crisis is a very good starting point for a company.

- In an analysis of the business situation, the IO perspective functions as a "macroscope"—an excellent instrument for creating an understanding of the operation as a whole and of what needs to be done.
- There are certain strategies for a company to start building an imaginary organization when it is not under the pressure of a challenge:

  1. Establish a subsidiary, build it up, and manage it as if it were part of an imaginary organization.

  2. Establish a "garage company", with competent employees who are younger than 30.

  3. Start a project based on a technology unfamiliar to company personnel.

- The IO perspective reveals the unique aspect of each party's contribution. This specialization by particular competence makes the IO more effective than traditionally organized operations. Each company focuses its development efforts on the qualities which make it unique, while the IO concentrates on developing mechanisms for innovation.

9
Focusing Strategy on Core Competence

Starting a new business with limited resources of your own; renovating and rejuvenating tired old enterprises "of no value"; growing into the infrastructure of others—these are situations in which an IO perspective leads to new discoveries that furnish new energy. The company operates in networks, strategic alliances, in which the business is an intercompany one based on symbiosis and joint use of resources. Using the concepts of core competence and applications, we can describe and understand this process.

CORE COMPETENCE AND ITS APPLICATIONS

Innovation and growth in active collaboration with other companies occur when each party controls and cultivates its core competence. The parties attract each other and achieve their positions by offering access to a core competence which is competitive compared to what others can offer, both within and outside the imaginary organization.

Core competence relates to the capacity to act to attain objectives. Knowledge of facts, skills, experience, values, attitudes, and networks contribute to our competence. The competence of a company is expressed through, and interwoven with, its technology, processes, and structures—but also in its ability to develop an attractive trademark, outlet location, and market position, and to use real assets like facilities, raw materials, and equipment.

A core competence can be identified (Prahalad, 1993) by the following test:

1. Does it permit differentiation in relation to competitors? Does it give the company a unique advantage or quality?
2. Is it broad enough to allow several applications?
3. Can it be protected from imitation by competitors?

To focus on core competence is to bring to light the company's history and its experience which has been accumulated over time in the form of capacity to perform certain activities. Porter (1985) identified five categories of primary value activities (inbound logistics; operations; outbound logistics; marketing and sales; service) and four categories of support activities (procurement; technology development; human resource management; and firm infrastructure). A company's competitive advantage is found in one or more of these. A core competence may be one source of such advantage. Some examples: Skandia emphasizes easy-to-use analytical tools that enable its partners to perform many of the tasks normally associated with an insurance business; GANT has developed a superiority in orchestrating the building of a particular image among its customers. Developing a core competence provides the foundation for the long-term development and growth of the company itself. It also may create a uniqueness that can be protected and refined over the years. Statements of business mission often focus on the customer interface: "to serve the X-market's need for Y-products". Such statements do not tell us anything about *why* our company should have any special success in attempting that. By focusing a core competence in one or a few value activities, we are closing in on the *raison d'être* of the lead company. Combining this talent with those of its partners, we may be able to create truly unique value constellations (cf. Normann & Ramirez, 1993.)

The parts of a company which customers see are the applications of its core competence in offers of products and services to different customer groups. The starting point for developing or describing an application is the customer and his situation. An offer is prepared for the customer in terms of product/service, price, information/obligations, and delivery. For each application the company develops a concept of business (what and for whom), a strategy, and a tactical marketing plan. The company organizes its resources/competence and develops systems for management control. To remain competitive, the company must constantly cultivate the product, adding new variations, removing old ones, and otherwise.

To summarize: we start with the customer and his situation when we develop applications. But what many companies have overlooked is to identify and develop the core competence which will assure their survival in the long run. When we specify a company's core competence, we begin—as noted above—with its history and experience. The time frame is long-range for the core competence, medium-range for concepts of business, short-range for individual varieties of products and services. For a company to be competitive in a market, the quality of its performance must be high in all of Porter's nine activities. Increasingly demanding requirements of functionality (a high know-how content) and flexibility make it virtually impossible for any company to perform all nine functions on its own. Collaboration becomes a necessity. Collaboration is often focused on an application, but seldom on the development of the core competence. The latter is something the company wants to keep to itself!

The companies which can identify their core competences and continually develops them are the ones which will be able to defend their position in a partnership over the long run.

ANALYSIS AND IDENTIFICATION OF THE COMMON FEATURES OF THE CASES

Position

Each of the companies we have described is the leader enterprise in its imaginary organization. Some were not leader enterprises at the outset, but succeeded in gaining that status. The people who started Grammofon AB BIS and Folkoperan had no leading position in the beginning. Only a few years ago, neither KalmarSalen, IMIT, nor the Värmdö Office of Cultural Affairs occupied the same leading position that they do today. (All case studies cited in this chapter are presented in greater detail in the Appendix.)

What makes a leader enterprise attractive to partners is its relationship with the customer base and its knowledge of what creates value for people *in their roles as customers*. Everyone in Sweden has on some occasion stopped at a Pressbyrån store. The unique knowledge of this enterprise about what creates value for us is limited to one particular situation in our lives: our stop at Pressbyrån. This knowledge is embodied in the expression "people on the go". The belief by partners in the ability of Pressbyrån to turn that knowledge into a concept of business makes the company attractive to both large and small suppliers.

Whether a company can maintain its position will depend on its ability to identify and cultivate its special core competence and to find applications for it that will create value for customers. Lorentzen & Wettre is an excellent example. That company knows it cannot compete with manufacturers of simple, low-price measuring instruments. Having chosen to serve demanding customers, the company identified its core competence as research and development in product control and process optimization in the world pulp and paper industry. By maintaining close contact with colleges and universities, by participating in the discussions of the research community, and by being close to customers, the company accumulates further knowledge for use in its own product-development projects.

The partners of Lorentzen & Wettre in component production are attractive if they can cultivate a core competence in cost-effective production. Those who continually improve their production methods will be included in the imaginary organization. In this manner companies gain and defend a leading position which commands the long-term confidence of both the customer base and the base of outside resources and competence. Since the company faces competition for its customers, loyalty to partners must be just sufficient to assure that they will continually do their utmost to improve performance. Subject to this limitation, the leader enterprise has the ability to create and maintain personal relationships with both existing and potential partner enterprises.

The imaginator

Without the power of the "imaginator" or IO-leader (see Chapter 1) to see opportunities within the reach of his company's core competence, there will be no innovation or growth. A clear picture emerged from the interviews with representatives of the companies in the case studies: at every leader enterprise there is a person or small group who hold the imaginary concept in their minds and develop it further. These people, the imaginators, share certain characteristics:

- An imaginator trusts the "involvees" (see Chapter 1).
- It makes little difference whether the involvees in a formal sense are employees of the imaginator's own company or of another company.
- An imaginator likes to work together with others. The idea of leading a company without boundaries appeals to him; the imaginator sees the company as an enterprise of unlimited resources.
- An imaginator communicates the common concept to involvees, thus giving the imaginary organization an image within and outside the leader enterprise.
- An imaginator sees such great benefits from the imaginary organization that he avoids petty bickering in each instance over who gets what. He tries to create "win–win" situations, in which each party contributes according to its ability and is rewarded in a manner which is reasonably fair in the long run.

The emergence of the imaginary organization

To judge from our case studies, imaginary organizations emerge from situations which have posed a serious challenge to a company and its management. Declining profitability, new technology, a competence gap, and competition for customers are examples of situations which have forced managements to think in new ways.

The situation is not the only driving force. The personality and values of leading figures are just as important. Ideas about other ways to do business have been budding in their minds, often from dissatisfaction with traditional modes of thinking and acting with respect to innovation and growth. Imaginators have readily viewed the resources and competence of outsiders as potentially available to their own companies. For all these reasons, an IO perspective has come naturally to these people in their search for solutions.

Frequently, the triggering factor has been a competence gap. At the risk of going a little too far, one may say that a lack of competence is the reason why companies run into trouble. A company may have failed to master an important new technology; it may be tardy in recruiting the people needed to maintain its competence in the long run; profits may be declining because of mismanagement. All these situations may be viewed as instances of a competence gap.

Still another force which appears to promote the emergence of the IO is the obligation of the managing director and other managers to achieve results. The ultimate responsibility of a managing director is to produce a satisfactory return on capital. Whether he does so with the company's own resources or by joint use of others' resources is of minor interest to the stockholders.

Management has two choices. One is the traditional approach of first upgrading the competence of the company's own employees—in CD-ROM technology, for example—and then moving on to commercial applications. The other is to begin directly with commercial applications and obtain the missing competence by co-operating with outside specialists. In our case studies, management has been able to assure long-term profitability by choosing the second alternative and thus saving valuable time.

The secret of successful leadership has been a subject of management research for over half a century. In the beginning the focus was on personal qualities. When no correlation could be found between personal qualities and success, researchers turned to the question of whether a good leader should be primarily people-oriented or task-oriented. Here, too, it proved difficult to establish a correlation.

More recent research has been devoted to the manner in which a leader responds to different situations. It has been found that leaders who can adapt their leadership style to the particular nature of each situation are more likely to be successful. Our analysis is quite consistent with this finding. The IO perspective is likely to result in success when the following factors are present:

- The company is facing a challenge, and the problem cannot obviously be solved by a traditional, "in-house" approach.
- The personality and values of company leaders are those of the imaginator, as described above.
- The task is clear and permits follow-up.

CORE COMPETENCE AS A BASE

For the leader enterprise to have something to offer, it must possess or acquire a unique competence which may take the form of a "recipe" for a certain technology or method, a customer data base, or a well-established reputation. It may also consist of skill in cultivating a network of contacts, and of the benefit of their personal confidence.

It is often a matter of selecting from, and cultivating, a legacy of the company's past. Fritzes and SCF are examples. In several of our case studies, the know-how was initially a talent of the imaginator. This pattern is particularly frequent in the creation of new enterprises. In the case of BIS and Folkoperan, the personal adroitness of the founders has improved even further with passing years. It remains to be seen whether the competence of these entrepreneurs has been institutionalized so that the imaginary organization could continue without them.

We usually think of a concept of business as focused on certain customer needs. In this sense, though, the imaginary concept is not necessarily the equivalent of the concept of the entire business; rather, it relates to the way in which the company's own competence fits into a larger arrangement, often one with several different applications. The competence creates added value. It gains leverage by borrowing from the competence of others.

In recent years the idea has emerged that the foundation of a company's various businesses is the strategic cultivation of its competence. This statement also applies to traditional companies. The concept of core competence was particularly emphasized by Prahalad and Hamel in a 1990 article in the *Harvard Business Review*. The core competence of an organization is the central foundation of its operations. Prahalad and Hamel (Hamel & Prahalad, 1994; Hamel & Heene, 1994) describe the company as a tree whose roots consist of different areas of competence. The trunk is formed by the company's core products. From it the business units branch out, bringing the end products to market.

An example: Recently, the Saab–Scania group split into Saab (aircraft and passenger cars, the latter jointly owned with GM) and Scania (trucks) after almost 50 years as one corporation. To many observers, Saab and Scania had never really merged internally. To justify the existence of the Saab group, and its collaboration with GM in passenger cars, a concept was needed to show how the group could cultivate the joint competence of several divisions, continually learning and transferring new competence from one division to the others. There is surely a cost of belonging to a corporate group—probably 1–2% of sales—so that there must be a corresponding benefit at least as great. Generating that benefit is the job of corporate management. More is required than just demanding a certain profit or return. The search for the right core competence is a matter of "intellectual leadership". Management must correctly guess what will be strategically decisive in the long run. It seems that in the end, Saab–Scania's group management decided that the synergies were not worth the effort (also see Goold et al, 1994).

We have found that several of the companies in our case studies were facing crucial decisions of this kind. What is really the core of Pressbyrån, of the Stockholm Stock Exchange, of Fritzes? How can management identify it? We have already asked critical questions about what should be viewed as the core competence of SAS.

RESOURCING INSTEAD OF OUTSOURCING

"Back to basics" and "focusing" have become watch-words in efforts to limit a company to activities of vital strategic importance and to areas in which it can be a winner or at least operate efficiently. Accordingly, it would be better to subcontract activities not part of this core (outsourcing), or even to discontinue them entirely and buy them from competing suppliers when necessary. Arguing that their companies must concentrate on the areas of its core competence, executives have phased out or sold certain product groups: the dataprocessing department has been replaced by an independent service center under a leasing agreement; a catering firm has taken over the employee dining room; the reception is manned by a guard from a security service. Not all trees have survived this pruning with their core and vitality intact.

But the identification of the core competence as described by Prahalad and Hamel serves primarily an offensive purpose rather than a defensive one. From time to time a company must clearly define its core competence as a platform for further growth. Proceeding from that definition, the company formulates its strategy and conducts a search for new products, services, and applications. Just as a good gardener prunes his fruit trees, selecting branches and buds for growth, excision, and grafting, good management draws on its understanding of the core competence to promote growth, achieve dominance, and make the company a winner. In this context *"resourcing"* is a more appropriate term than *"outsourcing"*.

A strategic architecture based on management's knowledge, on intracompany learning, and on learning from alliances with outside parties, provides the structure and the vision for growth. Our guesses as to what is strategically important are based on hypotheses about the future development of the industry. This aspect of business leadership often requires taking intellectual chances, betting on the kind of knowledge that will prove critical for success—and being able to cultivate that knowledge.

Companies in various sectors of the electronics industry provide an interesting example in this regard. What core competence can furnish a sustainable basis for persuading households to buy stereo and TV sets? Different companies follow different hypotheses. Some appear to favor new technical solutions (Philips), while others prefer attractive new applications and minimalization (Sony), and still others emphasize design (Bang & Olufsen). What you do not have yourself you can get from others, but you cannot be sure about what would work out. You can be even less sure about your best course of action. There may be unexpected consequences:

> If outsourcing is taken to the point where the locus of systems learning migrates to key suppliers, the tables could easily be turned, and the subcontractor could become the prime contractor, and *vice versa*. Thus it is conceivable that if electronics becomes critical in automobile technology and the present auto assemblers do not keep up, the design hierarchy could become inverted, with companies like GM, Ford, and Chrysler performing contract assembly for the electronics giants of tomorrow, who would then assume the role of systems integrator for automobiles. A similar scenario could unfold in commercial aircraft. (Teece, 1992, p. 192).

Thus, before we start building an imaginary organization, it is critical that we understand what core competence the leader enterprise possesses and is capable of developing further.

DO IT YOURSELF, SUBCONTRACT, OR BUILD?

Since the early 1900s the trend has been away from self-sufficient, fully integrated companies toward ones with an increasingly limited scope of activities and an ever greater dependence on subcontractors. Previously confined to industry, this trend has now spread to hospitals and school administration. It has been most clearly expressed in a book by Quinn (1992) *Intelligent Enterprise*. The author maintains that a company must make a deliberate strategic choice of what it intends to be good at. The company should compare itself with others in respect to every single function, keeping under its own roof only those at which it believes it can be the world champion. All other operations should be entrusted to others, who can perform them at less cost and/or better. It is difficult enough to be best in one's chosen field.

When we speak of the imaginator and the role of the leader enterprise in the imaginary organization, we are not talking about this kind of extensive use of subcontractors. We require more. The imaginator must also consider *how* the other parties involved in the IO can develop their competence and work together with his enterprise. In our IO concept, these issues are crucial! For example, a company may be facing a decision on whether to continue doing its own data-processing. A growing number of companies have created a data-processing subsidiary which they have sold a few years later. What you need is seldom unique and can usually be purchased from a number of facility providers. If you are not satisfied, you can switch to another one. Many computer-related services are rapidly becoming commodities interchangeable and widely available. In such areas, companies whose main activities are not data processing can hardly be competitive, and should look to outside suppliers.

There may be other reasons for the growing resort to subcontractors, and other aspects of the issue as well. We can think of certain important applications which are not like commodities and yet are too demanding for the necessarily limited competence and resources of our own data-processing department. However, we must not forget to consider the special nature of our business—a standardized solution will not do. We decide to collaborate with a data-consulting firm, but much more intimately. Each of us must seek to know the other better and to develop its own know-how with the prospect of a fairly long-run relationship in mind. Now we are using the perspective of the imaginary organization; as imaginators we must have carefully considered questions such as how to cultivate our relationship with the data-consulting firm, and how to influence the way it chooses to develop its own competence.

Lorentzen & Wettre appears to have such a relationship with some of its subcontractors. Still, the company refers to them as interchangeable. What degree of interdependence is desirable? A relationship may be only a strategic alliance, perhaps for collaboration on a specific project. We admit that the boundary may often be vague. Perhaps the test of an imaginary organization is whether the imaginator—intentionally or unintentionally—is following a strategy of cultivating competence along the lines of our present discussion. How can you influence the behavior of companies and individuals that do not formally belong to your company? When we start linking up our computers with those of suppliers or distributors, training their personnel, steering new business their way with the ulterior purpose of increasing their competence—clearly we no longer look at them as individual suppliers, each of which we hopefully gain from patronizing. Rather, we see an imaginator at work, managing his involvees to make the entire imaginary organization more effective.

Both the alliance and the imaginary organization are hybrids, utilizing elements of the market mechanism while answering to the command of a hierarchy, somewhere in-between the extremes of competition blind to loyalty and of blind obedience to plan. Probably the best description of the trade-offs involved has been furnished by Williamson (1975 and 1981). We referred in Chapter 2 to his statements on transaction costs: the market is preferable when the cost of co-ordination is low and competition leads to high efficiency. But the cost of finding suppliers, of telling them what you want, of inspecting what you get, and so forth, is sometimes very high. Hierarchy is then more economic.

The necessity to maintain a particular competence may also change over time. For many years, IKEA deliberately avoided manufacturing its furniture. However, with the company's growing involvement in joint ventures in Eastern Europe, a clear need arose for production know-how and for model factories which could serve as training schools for the foremen and workers at the Eastern European factories. Departing from its previous concept of business, IKEA purchased a small group of wood-processing companies in southern Sweden.

At times with great vigor, classical organization theorists used to debate the question of the optimal span of control—how many subordinates should report directly to a particular manager? With more refined systems and techniques of control, the span became larger. Today's modern information technology (LAN, groupware, Internet), has lowered transaction costs so drastically that the market can replace hierarchy in a number of new areas.

Reduced transaction costs thus permit effective co-ordination with a minimum of traditional hierarchy. Spontaneous lateral co-ordination of core competence between partner companies replaces the vertical co-ordination which formerly had to be managed through a hierarchy, by command or routine. How to create this internal market becomes an important question. Mutually beneficial relationships of exchange between leader and partner enterprises create an efficient trade in competence and resources, and the competitive power of the system as a whole becomes greater than it would have been with co-ordination by hierarchy. At the same time, however, new risks arise if the parties are not good enough at cultivating their relationships.

Hewlett-Packard and Apple each collaborated separately with Canon in developing a laser printer. Traditional thinking would have led each company to conclude that it had to develop the required know-how from within—in other words, provide the necessary co-ordination by hierarchy. The example also illustrates the downside risks of a strategic choice: while there was a contract not to compete, Canon introduced its own printer when the contract had expired.

If the imaginary organization is to last over the long run, all parties involved must find that they benefit from it. We have already referred to the issue of loyalty, to which we will return at several points below. While loyalty can rest on a number of different bases, it is best assured when the competence of the parties is complementary, so that they regard each other as indispensable.

KalmarSalen may be a relevant example. Local hotels are an essential part of the business. At the same time, a hotel may have its own network of contacts and consider itself as having its own imaginary organization which includes hotels at other locations. What the hotel learns from being associated with KalmarSalen may also be of value in its other business. Ties of this nature improve the odds that the system will last.

Sun Microsystems is a world leader in network computing with 17,000 employees. Products are manufactured in California and Scotland; research is done in the USA, France, Ireland, Japan and Russia; sales and support exist in 38 countries; and products are distributed in 100 countries.

Sun's *guiding management principles* are:

- Network
- Own core technology
- Leverage partnerships
- Sell Sun technologies through multiple channels
- Stable, well-managed, lean and effective business model

The central role given to "leverage partnerships" is highly interesting. "As much as we'd like every world-class person to work for Sun, we realized this is not going to happen", says the Director of Sun's Global Accounts Program. That's why partnerships are important. They exist for hardware and software, manufacturing, service, and distribution. There are also special partnerships for the development of interactive video (set-top boxes). These efforts are co-ordinated at group level using a 5-year perspective by a special team headed by the CIO.

The partnerships take different forms: from formal joint ventures (e.g. with Thomson), over contracts (Kodak and Bell Atlantic) to more temporary alliances. This mode of operation reflects Sun's origins in the academic community (as *Stanford University Network*). Partners may also be small, local firms: customers' day-to-day contacts with Sun may be through service employees who operate with Sun business cards, although they are in fact employed in other firms.

RECOGNIZING CORE COMPETENCE

In a way, the concept of the imaginary organization is a departure from the prevailing strategic recipe of recent years. Focusing on the customer and adapting to the market are not enough. To have something to offer, we must have cultivated the right competence, and for that purpose we must plan ahead. If our success is to last, we must keep on cultivating what we already have. We can reduce the risk of wasting our time on the wrong competence if we do not try to do everything ourselves but seek to influence others to help us.

On the market there will be battles between various IOs and other, more conventional, fully integrated companies. The vision, or imaginary concept, of some will endure better than that of others. We believe that to a growing extent the IO will win out because it permits flexibility and favors creativity. The arrangement of involvees can be readjusted and kept "porous", open to ideas brought in from other fields and other imaginary organizations in which involvees may also operate and where they can also develop their competence. In our case studies most of the involvees spend only a limited portion of their time working for the system in focus. Often the relationship is dormant for long periods. But the parties stay in touch, and they know what to expect of each other.

The IO concept is first and foremost a perspective, and a very powerful one. As the name suggests, it calls for creativity and imagination. We will later show that applying the concept not only can result in specific action; it can also produce a rather subtle form of leadership which the imaginator exercises without the support of a formal position of command. In every imaginary concept there is also a substantial degree of risk. The imaginator must be able to develop his own competence, link it to the competence of others, influence those others so that concepts of business can be developed and put into practice, and obtain a reward from a market where—after so much careful preparation—the system has succeeded in offering a product/service that meets customer needs.

Identifying potential core competence is largely a question for the imaginator. While inspiration is a creative act, in existing organizations it can be given some help along the way. For this purpose it can be useful to have a language and some maps that depict imaginary organizations.

Another approach is suggested by Porter (1985) and Quinn (1992), to whom we referred at the beginning of this Chapter. Using some form of benchmarking, we identify our relative superiority or inferiority in various activities and functions. This process calls for preparing flow charts, calculating costs, and determining the nature and quality of what is provided. It has become popular to speak of value chains, business process re-engineering, and similar terms. It all boils down to finding intelligent answers to questions about what needs to be done and what part of it we should do ourselves.

We are thinking primarily of the company's production of goods or services. But valuable competence is frequently found in auxiliary functions often referred to as "overheads" and reported as an indirect cost in the income statement; examples would be administration and development. A lot happens along the flow of production: development of methods, training, formation of data banks, on-going contact with actual and potential customers, etc. Often a company could operate at substantially lower cost by avoiding activities like these, but they may be justifiable for strategic reasons if they are part of the company's efforts to cultivate its heritage of competence.

Management thus has a starting point for discussing what can be expected to be critical in the future, or more properly: what would be reasonable to bet on for the future? The choice must be credible in terms of company competence. It may involve building further in some area where the company has already established a position, perhaps even unintentionally as a by-product of previous strategic choices. Tom Peters (1984) has spoken of a company's repertory of action, as if the company were a musical group, ballet ensemble or football team. An objective study might conclude that two companies (or groups of musicians, for example) currently have the same competence, but their previous experience with a particular repertory (musical compositions, styles of dancing, football plays) would make a difference in their capacity to develop new competence.

A credible imaginary concept also calls for an ability to influence involvees and perhaps to make collaboration and competence more permanent by introducing computerized solutions or procedures. In extreme cases the imaginary concept itself revolves largely around this kind of brokering talent. Here it is worth considering Richard Normann's (1984) classic example of service management: EF (an institute offering young people the opportunity to study abroad). In that instance, the prospect of collaboration was attractive to various involvees, who were just waiting for someone to link them together. If EF as a broker also begins to protect its network of teachers, host families, etc. by giving them a sense of participation, cultivates their competence by training them and enabling them to share their experience, etc., we then have an excellent case of an imaginary organization. On the other hand, if we are content to remain a broker and consider these parties interchangeable, we would regard them as subcontractors rather than involvees in our sense of the term, and it would be wrong to speak of an imaginary organization. We would be dealing with an ordinary business concept which lacked an essential distinguishing feature of the imaginary organization: cultivating the respective competence of co-operating parties.

It might be appropriate to consider some of our case studies in this light. Should Fritzes become more active in selecting its authors to fit the requirements of a particular publication? How strongly should IMIT's project managers exercise their leadership, by comparison with the practice of various local colleges and universities?

GAINING LEVERAGE FOR YOUR OWN COMPETENCE

As we have stated, a skillful leader enterprise deliberately cultivates the competence of involvees and of their enterprises. Their opportunity to develop is an important aspect of the imaginary organization. In a simple market solution, in which the agreement between the leader enterprise and partner enterprises may be terminated at any time, each party would use its negotiating position to squeeze concessions out of the other. In the imaginary organization both parties should feel that they profit by the relationship. Know-how is a good thing in itself and enlarges the pie to be shared by doing business together. Over time, involvees are presented with larger and more profitable business opportunities, both within and outside the IO. For this reason they are willing to relinquish some of their short-term objectives.

To realize this scenario, the imaginator must have the talent of a theatrical director. Failure may lead to attempts to extract unreasonable concessions, or involvees may feel used and pull out. The possibility that parties may put pressure on each other should be foreseen by the imaginator in drawing the boundaries between the competence of the leader enterprise and that of the partners. Recall the example of Hemglass (see Chapter 2), in which the distributors withdrew from the arrangement.

Another factor in deciding what functions to entrust to others is the skill of the leader enterprise in exercising influence outside its own formal organization and in creating mutually beneficial co-operative arrangements. If conditions are favorable, and the leader enterprise is skillful enough, an IO solution will be a real possibility, even where the risk of conflict and undue pressure might otherwise be considered too great.

If we succeed, we obtain leverage for our own competence. We use the term in the same sense as in business finance: borrowing gives a company leverage on the owners' equity. As in finance, there are also risks, but of a somewhat different kind. Borrowed money must be repaid with interest. As long we can earn a return higher than the rate of interest, as owners we pocket the difference, but if our return is less than the rate of interest, we have to put up the difference or go bankrupt. In other words, we should only be entrusted with other people's money if we can manage it better than the owners could by themselves. For them, the interest they receive is a satisfactory return; as for us, we borrow because we believe we can make their money earn more. If we succeed, it is tempting to operate with high leverage—that is, a high proportion of borrowed money—as expressed in the following well-known formula:

$$R_E = R_T + (R_T - R_D) \cdot D/E$$

in which R_T is our return on the total capital we employ (that is, the capital we have borrowed from others = debt, plus the capital we have invested ourselves = equity), R_D is the interest we pay on our debt, and D/E is the debt/equity ratio. The result is the return on our equity, R_E.

Similarly, when we bring the competence of others into our business, we give leverage to our own competence, thus increasing its usefulness—and our reward. But we will only succeed if the enterprise as a whole yields a better return than what the providers of borrowed competence would have obtained on their own. If it does, the more we borrow, the more we earn—but also, the greater the risk if we fail to achieve a higher return.

The parallel should not be stretched too far. The return on financial capital is a matter of investing and earning money and of sharing risk. As for sharing the return, it is a zero-sum game; if creditors receive more, there is less left for the owners. By contrast, the imaginary organization works best if it is useful to the participants in several different ways. If the benefits desired by the parties are varied in nature, everyone may feel that he has obtained greater leverage on his input.

The leverage for the core competence of the leader enterprise is indicated by the I/E ratio, where I stands for the number of involvees in the entire imaginary organization and E for the number of employees of the leader enterprise. I/E has a similar role as D/E in the formula above. Generally, however, the leader enterprise must take a more active part in the relationship with involvees, than the borrower with his creditors. We can borrow money on an impersonal market, but when we want others to make their competence available to us, we have to deal with them as people. A formal contract is seldom sufficient. We must try to instill in our involvees a sense of interdependence and commitment—what happens to them affects us, and *vice versa*. The imaginators in our case studies have apparently realized this necessity; they seem to regard personal relationships as particularly important. We will return to this subject in the next chapter.

Personal contacts are easy to manage in a small, new, imaginary organization, particularly for an active and extrovert imaginator. The chances for success increase with the number of natural synergies. If the participating companies right from the start have complementary assets in the form of a customer base, an established system of market communication, input goods, store locations, systems of delivery, production, or purchasing, then the imaginary concept is self-evident. But often someone must intervene to create the right incentives for all parties. In several of our case studies, we have seen how the imaginator himself has managed such a situation very adeptly, but at the expense of potential leverage. In spite of what we have said about how information technology can lower the cost of co-ordination, there is a limit to the number of personal contacts which a single imaginator can entertain. It is easy to resort to hierarchies and middle managers as a solution. Of course, a high I/E ratio is possible if all employees act as leaders and cultivate contacts with involvees. The model then resembles a corporate management team without a corporate structure.

Often, however, only a few persons in the leader enterprise share the imaginary concept. If they are to handle all involvee contacts, collaboration must be given more of a structure. We find a similar phenomenon in conventional corporate groups which today often seek to reduce the number of hierarchical levels. The inevitable result is a broader span of control—that is, more people report to each manager. The solution is believed to lie in clearer objectives and greater use of routine for necessary contacts. Thus, contacts of a more personal nature can be reserved for discussing exceptions and innovation.

Consequently, it will become necessary to develop more *structural capital*. By that term we mean procedures, customs, and particularly computer software, data bases, and the routines associated with using them. These will make the entire structure less dependent on the know-how of individuals. The fact that the contribution of the various involvees to the imaginary organization as a whole is based on their personal knowledge, should not prevent people from gradually learning to manage collaboration in a manner which can be documented and made permanent. In this way large numbers of involvees can receive information at the same time, so that the I/E ratio can be increased without over-loading the core of the system, the leader enterprise. This reasoning is presented graphically in Figure 9.1.

The cost of developing a comprehensive system of structural capital with a low I/E ratio is probably prohibitive in terms of

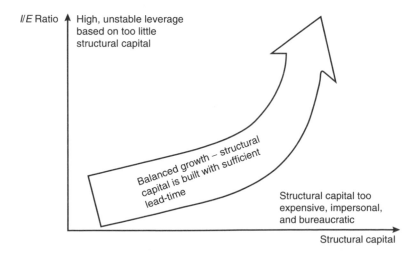

Figure 9.1 The need for structural capital

time as well as money. Such a system may also be perceived as unnecessarily bureaucratic—involvees expect more direct contact with the imaginator or his/her closest associates. But to make it possible to achieve a higher I/E ratio, structural capital is essential. The same is true when a large company is about to be renovated.

Herein lies the basis for the discussion in the USA on virtual organizations. Product development and continuous adaptation in response to signals from the market must engage an entire network of subcontractors. An automatic flow of information, planned in advance, is indispensable. At the same time, people are talking about how alliances should shift over time. We are not so sure that we agree. In our view, what primarily distinguishes the imaginary organization from a network of subcontractors is the jointly cultivated competence of the IO in working together.

10

Cultivating the Involvees

INTRODUCTION

We have previously defined "involvees" as all persons in the service of the imaginary organization (IO). The term includes, but is not limited to, the permanent employees of the leader enterprise. In fact, it is broader still; an involvee may also be another company, or a network of companies and/or individuals.

The concept of "involvee" is highly relevant in today's business world, in which companies and other organizations operate in systems, including the IO, which are becoming increasingly flexible and loosely connected. One of the images used to describe what is happening is the four-leafed clover (Shamrock) (Handy, 1989) Figure 10.1. Companies choose only their own employees for the core of the business. The rest is purchased from other parties—co-suppliers—or performed as necessary by temporary employees. Permanent employees, or core personnel, are becoming fewer, while a growing proportion of people work for companies as independent contractors or temporary employees.

Co-suppliers, for example, may be individuals or a group of involvees who collaborate to offer products or services to a company. The collaboration between the core company and its co-suppliers is long-lasting. Temporary employees may perform many different functions, from the simple to the complex. They differ from permanent employees and co-suppliers in not being an integral part of the business. They are readily interchangeable.

Figure 10.1 Shamrock organization

In the IO, the permanent employees of the leader enterprise are far outnumbered by the other involvees—those on a longer-term basis like partners or co-suppliers, and those on a temporary basis who are brought in as needed. In fact, these other involvees may be associated with the leader enterprise in many different ways: as co-suppliers, partners, project associates, or persons temporarily engaged for a particular purpose. Therefore, what we refer to as the I/E ratio is very high in the imaginary organization. The I/E ratio is equal to the total number of involvees (including employees of the leader enterprise) in the business of the IO, divided by the number of employees of the leader enterprise alone. In all of our case studies, the I/E ratio of the imaginary organization is considerably greater than 1. In traditional companies it is typically not much more than 1.

- *Skandia AFS.*   Some 60 persons work at headquarters. An additional 2300 Skandia employees run the national companies, but these people engage some 70,000 partners in various countries. The partners include money managers, financial consultants, and major savings banks.

$$I/E = 70,000/2300 = 30$$

- *Folkopera.*   Has seven employees, of whom three or four are permanent. Other involvees are engaged on a project basis and can number over 500.

$$I/E = 507/7 = 72.$$

- *The Värmdö Office of Cultural Affairs.*   The number of permanent positions at the Office is the equivalent of only 2.5 full-time employees. But approximately 100 other people are involved: contacts at associations and educational federations, school officials responsible for the arts, various co-operative organizations, enthusiastic volunteers, etc.

$$I/E = 102.5/2.5 = 41.$$

WINNING LOYALTY BY OFFERING DEVELOPMENT OF COMPETENCE

More and more people have a personal strategy of working for companies and other organizations which can offer them employability—by assuring the renewal of their competence and thus maintaining their attractiveness on the labor market. They exchange employment security for employability, a guarantee more reliable than any promises of a safe job.

Employability is created by continually renewing and developing one's competence. Unlike many traditional companies, with their closed systems and inflexible work procedures, the imaginary organization is quite appropriate for harnessing the ambitions of people interested in employability. The IO benefits from their skills and provides a platform for a growing number of them to build up a personal portfolio of assignments and customers.

At companies with an I/E ratio close to 1, employees are tied to the company by employment contracts. Underlying these contracts is an assumption of employment security and life-long employment in exchange for the company's right to direct and divide the work. The conditions of the contract relate to the position held and the time to be spent at work. In the imaginary organization most personnel are not employees but are associated with the business under commercial contracts which specify expected results. Compensation is not only financial; also important is enhancement of employability and eligibility for new assignments. In large measure the contract is invisible in that it is based on mutual trust in the other's performance and contribution to value and development of competence.

TRUST

In imaginary organizations, an important function of the leader of the IO is to create trust between employees and involvees as well as among different involvees. The question is how to ensure that a

Table 10.1 Comparison between the employment contract of a company and the commercial contract between partners

	Employment contract	Commercial contract
Focus	Position	Task/assignment
Rewarded for	Time at work	Results
Responsible	The boss	The individual
Trust	Loyalty to the company	Loyalty to the task (customer) and the network

large number of involvees, most of whom are not employees, will care about what happens to the business as a whole.

Trust is based on loyalty, which is built up through a continuing dialog between the leader enterprise and the involvees, as well as among the involvees. It is reinforced when expectations are met and when the rewards received by the parties are in balance.

Loyalty should be sufficient but not excessive; it must also be given a means of expression. If involvee loyalty knows no bounds, management may not bother to listen. If it is insufficient, involvees may be too quick to leave instead of trying to change the enterprise. We have previously discussed Exit and Voice (see Chapter 2) as means of expression. An employee or other involvee may resort to Voice—the system of information, meetings, etc.—to gain the attention of management. If he/she is unable to do so, the Exit option remains: he/she can leave the enterprise. Exit and Voice are ways of putting pressure on management to change.

There must be a clear image of objectives, an exciting, unifying vision, of the *entire* imaginary organization. There must also be an adequate forum for the exercise of Voice (ideas, differences of opinion) throughout the system. Employees and other personnel must care enough about the well-being of the business to think about and get involved in its future.

- *Skandia AFS.* CEO Jan Carendi says that in order to lead the company he has to realize that he is managing a "voluntary association". To keep the Skandia AFS network together, he attempts to create a challenging vision, provide fast feedback on performance, and nourish a "high-trust culture". Everyone in this voluntary organization must be a "trustee", someone who deserves the trust of others and who trusts his/her collaborators.

- *Liber–Hermods.* Liber–Hermods makes a conscious effort to cultivate relationships with teachers and textbook writers. Teachers receive training and must never be dissatisfied with the support provided by the materials furnished to them. A relationship with a writer is like a marriage.
- *KalmarSalen.* It is important to provide involvees with information and sales arguments. Involvees are given the limelight when negotiations for new arrangements have been successfully concluded.
- *The Värmdö Office of Cultural Affairs.* This organization gives an annual "staff party" to which it invites not only employees but all involvees, from personal contacts in different organizations to enthusiastic volunteers.

IDEAS FOR ENCOURAGING INVOLVEMENT

Many companies must constantly renew the competence and motivation of their employees, who are so essential to their whole business. At the same time, the company must meet varying employee needs. Many employees would like to see their jobs as a way of developing their talents and not just of making a living. It is important to see that persons involved in various ways in an IO business can maintain and develop their attractiveness and employability/eligibility for other engagements.

To be successful over an extended period, an IO must match up the needs of the business and those of the involvees in a mutually beneficial arrangement. "The involvees are the most important asset of the IO". But the converse must also be true: "The IO is the most important asset of the involvees".

A depleted capital stock may cause the liquidation of a corporation. There is a certain analogy between depletion of capital stock and depletion of the motivation and competence of employees and other involvees of the imaginary organization. The enterprise which consumes more than it adds to the competence of its personnel is setting the stage for failure.

The imaginary organization should have a well-considered and well-expressed concept of how to attract and develop its human resource. It must specify what employees and other involvees are required (competence and needs), and also what is required to recruit them, to get them to stay on, to motivate them, and to develop their competence—in short, a human resource strategy.

- *Skandia AFS.* The following are extracts from the company's Statement of Core Values:

    Role of the individual—You are responsible for your own growth based on an understanding of the AFS philosophy and mission, cultivation of partnerships, and willingness to invest for the future.

    Leadership—By leadership at Skandia AFS we mean care of customers, care of people actively seeking partnership and innovation, and developing and utilizing competence, as demonstrated by our own example and initiatives.

    Organization—We will promote continuous innovation by learning and teaching through utilizing established units for rapid transfer of competence and experience in a growing global federation.

- *SCF.* Involvees of SCF must be independent consultants with a separate practice. They should enjoy participating in a common development effort and should be capable of working in a group.
- *Folkopera.* Many artists join Folkopera for a particular production, leave afterwards for another production elsewhere, and come back later. Learning from each engagement, they develop their competence. Folkopera is the better for it.

Human resource strategies and policies must include all participants throughout the IO, not just the employees. It is wrong to exclude a large category of "personnel" from the staff party just because they are not employees.

TIES BETWEEN THE IMAGINARY ORGANIZATION AND ITS INVOLVEES

Involvees are dependent on the IO in varying degrees; the converse is also true. Since the strength of these ties can vary, so must the strategies for the choice of contractual arrangement and the nature of the involvement.

Each party has its conception of the competence and kind of involvement required, and of the degree to which these factors are critical for success. The more specific and critical the competence and the involvement—to the business and to the future of the individual—the stronger the ties between him/her and the IO.

As previously stated, the needs of the imaginary organization may be expressed in a concept of personnel which includes all involvees. The needs of the individual may be expressed as a concept of professional career. While neither of these ideas is usually very well articulated, they should be to facilitate a dialog on mutual expectations and matching of needs. Individuals would then be required to discuss their career progress, to keep track of it, and to compare it with their goals.

The competence and involvement of employees and other involvees can be described in terms of their specificity and criticality to the performance of the imaginary organization. The converse is true as well.

The degree of difficulty in specifying and measuring the necessary competence also varies, thus greatly affecting the nature of the ties between the involvees and the system.

If the competence required to match a particular need is not critical to the core competence, and if it is easy to measure, it can be purchased when needed. No special ties are called for; detailed contracts can be drafted to formalize mutual expectations. For the IO, the other parties may be individuals involved more or less temporarily, or they may be companies of various kinds. The relationship is maintained as long as both parties are satisfied with the results; there is no depth to it, since each party is highly interchangeable for the other.

The left-hand column in Figure 10.2 represents situations like these. In the lower row it is difficult to measure individual contribution in terms of hours worked or number of units produced. The agreement will then be broader in scope or cover a certain period. The right-hand column shows the opposite situation. The competence required is critical to the core competence. The same is true from the individual's point of view. What he/she does in the system is important for the development of his/her own competence. Quite possibly, the individual's competence cannot be used elsewhere. The parties are mutually dependent and will do all they can to continue the contract.

Persons with competence that is easy to show and measure may be regarded as permanent involvees without the status of employees.

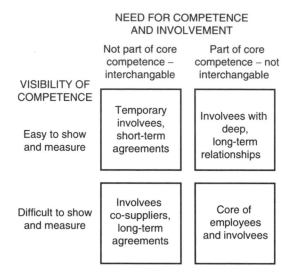

Figure 10.2   Different kinds of ties

Involvees can participate in the imaginary organization as part of their personal portfolio of engagements and customers. The contract with the leader enterprise may cover a service, a particular competence, or a product.

When the competence and involvement of several persons must be interwoven in a larger whole, it becomes difficult to identify the contribution of each. In such a case a core is established, consisting of employees and other involvees who are associated on similar terms. Some have employment contracts, while others have contracts relating to a particular business project or competence.

CONTRACTS

The relationships between management and employees and involvees are governed by some form of agreement or contract. In several of our case studies, the companies had a very informal approach to contracts.

- *SCF*. The purpose of not having contracts is to keep the focus on the dialog between the Association and the various involvees. In the dialog we can create the mutual trust we need.

The unwritten contracts are more important than the written ones, which concern a particular business project or competence. The agreements call for a specific service, a specific result, maintenance of a specific competence, etc.

The relationship covers more than a single commercial transaction, in which considerations of loyalty would normally play little part. In the imaginary organization, efforts are made to find mutually beneficial and profitable forms of co-existence over a longer period. Both parties to a business contract are generally aware of the potential for other business in the future. The IO leader and the leader enterprise try to turn this possibility to the advantage of both parties.

It appears that the form and content of the contract is highly dependent on the importance of the relationship between the involvee and the imaginary organization. Short-term employment or supply contracts (see the left-hand column in Figure 10.2) may be relied on if the competence required is interchangeable and not critical, and if it is easy to determine the quality of performance.

Contracts tend to cover longer periods when quality can be measured, but the competence required is specially adapted to the needs of the system and is critical to it or to the individual. Such contracts may provide for rewards which are withheld until "loyalty" has been manifested, the individual has been offered a firm plan for the development of his/her personal competence, etc. (see the upper right-hand corner of Figure 10.2).

When there is a high degree of interdependence among several involvees whose contributions are critical to the outcome, it is also necessary to include them in the culture and management of the enterprise (see the lower right-hand corner of Figure 10.2).

- *SCF.* A contract is necessary but not sufficient. The contract is one thing; co-operation is another. It is important to establish various forms of mutual dependence and exchange.
- *IMIT.* The critical resource in IMIT consists in the long-term personal relationships which have been established with researchers at the founding institutions. The critical function is to give IMIT an image to outsiders and to involvees. It is important to communicate the common concept to employees and other involvees, particularly the researchers. The latter are a critical resource, and there is stiff competition for their services.

How much should be specified in formal contracts? It is sometimes a matter of tradition. Obligations may be unspoken or established by custom. Sometimes they may be interpreted differently by different parties. We need only look to everyday life for examples. Do we expect a store to order goods which we have been unable to find? Do we feel obligated to come back to buy them? Have we failed to meet a commitment if we go to another store where we can get the items at a lower price?

In fields where outsourcing has become widespread, as in computer services, we find examples of the difficulties encountered when the parties have tried both to be extremely specific about what is covered by the contract and to create a basis for a long-term relationship of trust. Outsourcing, or opening the provision of a service to competition, makes it very hard to define in a contract what is meant by quality. Human psychology being what it is, this area has a high potential for disputes and for attracting advice of varying quality. We have also heard the view that cautious lawyers can have an inhibiting effect on the development of an imaginary organization.

MEASURING THE BENEFIT

The competence and involvement of employees and other involvees are at the heart of the business and constitute all of the essential value of many imaginary operations. Reports on financial performance are not enough; the signals they give us are too slow in coming. It is at least as important to find ways to measure and monitor involvement and the development of competence; they can give us an early indication of whether the business is on the right track.

In large-scale imaginary organizations, both the enterprise and the involvees need methods and tools for measuring performance. The leader enterprise must be able to see whether competence and involvement are developing as intended, and to make sure that the needs of the enterprise remain consistent with those of the involvees.

In small imaginary organizations there is of course little need for highly technical methods. The IO-leader and the various involvees work closely together, so that all of them can see how the business is doing and whether contractual requirements are being met.

What is easiest to measure may not necessarily show whether the right course of action has been taken. A one-sided focus on what can be measured directly in monetary terms may lead to the wrong decision. As often in the case of competence and involvement, these objective measures of value should be supplemented by subjective ones, such as satisfaction and the sense that one's competence has been affirmed.

In describing the benefit of involvement in an IO, one may consider a scale of values based on a theory developed by Robert Hartman (1967). He distinguishes three different methods of evaluation and levels of value:

1. *Inner values* (emotional, intellectual), such as attitudes, workplace atmosphere, willingness to change, ability, involvement, relationships.

2. *Outer values* (practical, functional), such as efficiency, productivity, abundance of ideas, market share, absenteeism, involvee turnover, sales per involvee, number of network contacts.

3. *System values*, such as higher revenues, lower costs, salary increases.

It is possible to measure value at each level. Inner values are often measured on a scale of some kind, showing attitudes, emotions, and level of skill, for example. Outer values are expressed as key ratios, such as employee turnover. Key ratios are meaningful only when compared with established goals or over time. System values can be measured in absolute terms like dollars or sterling.

Our case studies have given us the impression that for the exchange between an IO-leader and other involvees to be productive, to further the development of both parties, and to endure, it must attain a level at which inner values are created. Probably it must include all three levels if it is to be fruitful. Inner values take precedence over outer ones, which in turn take precedence over system values.

Human-resource accounting

Many companies today are attempting to use so-called human-resource accounting. They are assuming that the effects of various actions concerning personnel translate directly into system values, which are monetary, or into outer values like key ratios. Important measures of value in human-resource accounting also include employee turnover and absence due to illness. Actions taken concerning human resources are treated just like other investments; the outcome is measured in the same way and subject to the same kinds of uncertainty as marketing investments, investments in the form of acquiring other companies, and the like.

For the imaginary organization, measures of this kind are also useful, but employee turnover becomes an analysis of involvee turnover. Time spent on development of competence is probably more interesting than absenteeism from illness.

In an IO it is important to be able to measure what involvees contribute to revenue, particularly when we evaluate their involvement and the development of their competence. However, we also want to know their contribution in the form of new ideas, innovative capacity, and ability to establish and maintain networks of contacts. Contributions to increased revenue must be measured along an entire scale of value, and competence, for example, can also be measured in this way.

Table 10.2 Various ways of measuring competence

Area of competence	Examples of indirect measures of competence
Knowledge	Level of education (system value) Proportion of involvees familiar with IT (outer value)
Experience	Number of years in the profession (system value) Proportion of involvees with experience in … (outer value)
Skills	Number of years in the profession (system value) Number of proposals presented/year (outer value)
Networks	Number of different units where you have worked (system value) Number of outside engagements (system value) Attitude toward co-operation (inner value)
Value judgments	Opinions about the business (inner value) Attitude toward innovation (inner value)

The balanced scorecard

It is becoming increasingly important to find a way to measure inner values and to learn to interpret them directly. There is no need to translate them into system values expressed in monetary terms. The large imaginary organizations which we have studied use inner values in parallel with system values. Opinions, evaluations, and judgments by customers, employees, and other involvees are shown on scales together with rates of return, sales volumes, and financial results. Various kinds of knowledge about attitudes are important in an imaginary operation. Systematic information must be gathered by a variety of methods, from various forms of discussion to systematically conducted attitude studies.

- *Skandia AFS.* At Skandia AFS a Balanced Scorecard called "Navigator" has been developed as a means of monitoring what is happening in the business, not only financial performance but above all in the growth of intellectual capital. Progress is measured under different headings: Financial Focus; Customer Focus; Process Focus; and Innovation and Development Focus. The latter three provide important ways to measure Skandia's intellectual capital, which is also the core of the business.

  From this balanced scorecard for the business as a whole, a personal scorecard for employees and other involvees has also been developed. The personal scorecard permits each individual to follow his/her progress and benefit. The card provides the user with various measures for evaluating the state of the relationship between the leadership and the people involved in the system. Examples include the following:

  - Involvee's own value added.
  - Measures of employability, or development of competence.
  - Number of network contacts.
  - Number of proposals presented.
  - Time spent on development of competence.
  - Trust.

A personal Balanced Scorecard provides a good basis for an individual to follow his/her progress and contribution to the development of the common enterprise. It can also be used to monitor the progress of relationships with people in different networks.

SUMMARY

Relationships between the leader enterprise, employees, and other involvees must not be allowed to become a zero-sum game. All parties involved must find that their benefit from working together exceeds what they must contribute. Therefore, the IO-leader must understand the kind of relationship to be sought, the importance of collaborating, and what the various parties might want to obtain by doing so.

All parties at the core of the imaginary organization must feel that the benefit which they receive not only is financial but also contributes to their own development. Trust among involvees must create inner value if it is to be strong enough to hold the imaginary organization together.

In small imaginary operations the leader, who works closely with all involvees, can directly follow the development of trust, involvement, and competence. In larger businesses control ratios are needed to show whether progress is being made in the right direction. The personal balanced scorecard is one way that works.

11
Management Control

In Chapter 9 the idea was introduced that the leader enterprise of the imaginary organization borrows the competence of others to obtain a better result from its own, in much the same way as an ordinary company borrows money to improve the leverage on its stockholders' equity. The essential point is that the borrower understands how to use others' resources better than the owners could have themselves. The odds of success can be improved by appropriate communication between the leader and its partners concerning objectives and measures of performance. How can this communication be designed? What agreements are needed on sharing the results of collaboration?

LEVERAGE, MEASUREMENT, AND OBJECTIVES

By tradition, economics at the company level is largely a matter of measuring resources in monetary terms and of dividing the monetary surplus among different parties. In the imaginary organization, economics in the sense of *effective management of resources* should concern more than money. Viewed as a management responsibility, economics is about cultivating and developing different kinds of resources. Obtaining higher leverage by co-operating with others belongs to this domain.

The concept of *management control* has become generally accepted as a term for the manner in which an organization uses accounting information for internal control. The term includes cost/benefit analysis, investment appraisal and managerial accounting, with a growing emphasis on the purposeful use of information to determine the direction which the business should take. In the imaginary organization, the boundary between external and internal becomes less clear.

It is important to use scarce resources efficiently, to cultivate them better, to develop them better, and to obtain better leverage on their use. What are those resources in the imaginary organization, and what information can we provide about them? Naturally, we are referring to the competence and all related factors which are important for making the imaginary concept work: various kinds of know-how, customer relationships, and structural capital. Thus, we are also talking about *measuring assets and using resources other than money*: appropriate indicators may include quantities produced, percentage personnel turnover, store of knowledge, number of customers served exclusively by us, etc.

Controllers are accustomed to data that primarily measure what is happening inside a company. But now information on the company's market shares, for example, is often found in the same reports as revenues and expenses. Perhaps market-share targets should also be included in the budget. Thus, the boundaries between the information systems of managerial accounting and those of other departments such as marketing are being eroded. In the imaginary organization there is an analogous erosion of boundaries between the information systems of different companies.

While we are mainly referring to quantitative measures, sometimes other forms of managerial accounting data are used. For example, verbal comments on actual results compared to budget are also of interest to managers. Information of common interest to the involees in the imaginary organization might include measurements and descriptions of quite a different kind.

The *tools* of the controller which we have in mind are classic ones: costing, budgets, internal income statements—which often require some form of transfer pricing, etc. What interests us is how these tools facilitate control and are necessary for its exercise. If collaboration in the imaginary organization is to be formalized through a joint computer system, substantial investments in time and money will be called for.

The traditional perspective on management control is orientated toward rational problem solving. Estimates and budgets are presented as analytical tools for determining the correct course of action under given assumptions about the future. In real-life organizations, it is more fruitful to emphasize *communication among different actors*. The design of information for management control affects their interaction. The manner of designing a management-control system is a subtle but powerful way to affect what happens. Particularly in non-hierarchical structures like the imaginary organization, we can exert a major controlling influence by consciously choosing how we design the flow of information.

Therefore, the perspective of this chapter emphasizes the processes and content of communication, especially in more formalized and purposefully designed procedures. Since controllers and managerial accountants influence these procedures and participate in them, their roles are undergoing change.

The central concept here is *managerial responsibility*: who is in charge of what, and how do we ensure that the various people in charge perform as intended, on their own and in relation to each other? In the imaginary organization, controllers have no hierarchical power structure to fall back on. Either there is no hierarchy at all, or if there is one, it is the product of a voluntary and selective agreement.

Management control in the sense described above is exercised in conjunction with other forms of control, primarily the division of labor provided for by various kinds of organizational structures, and the prevailing culture (shared ideas, company spirit, atmosphere . . .). A successful system of management control both complements these other forms of control and is compatible with them. The imaginary organization is often highly dependent on a consensus around values and objectives. This consensus must find support in the way performance is measured by the system of management control.

Like other forms of control, management control presupposes the existence of *goals*, or at least an indication of the direction to be followed. This requirement stems partly from needs common to all organizations. Ordinarily, these needs include survival, which for a company implies certain threshold levels of liquidity and profitability. But the more conscious and deliberate we are in allocating responsibility and in designing the system of communication, the clearer we must be about where we want to go. If we are to make efficient use of the tools of management control, we must have answers to questions about intentions, objectives, and purpose. At many companies, management has not formulated its answers.

What we have said up to this point is true of all organizations, or at least larger ones where it is possible to allocate responsibility among a number of smaller units. However, even smaller organizations may benefit from this approach to management control, and some do employ the tools of management control for that purpose. In a world in which it is important to use resources efficiently, our actions are strongly influenced by managerial accounting data.

MANAGEMENT CONTROL

For our purposes the subject of management control is wide-ranging; it includes such areas as legal contracts and formal structure of ownership. These also build on structured use of information about the economic resources of the firm, and the economic outcomes of its actions. Consequently, the term is not limited to managerial accounting and internal control. What is internal in the imaginary sense is often external in the legal sense, because the leader enterprise has chosen to regard other legal entities besides itself as part of its imaginary organization.

We find a parallel in a number of major Swedish corporate groups, which draw a distinction between legal and operating control. The legal structure of the group includes numerous companies, one reason being that it is most natural to conduct foreign operations through separate companies. For purposes of control, however, another structure is preferred, such as a divisional one; the management of each company is thus encouraged to achieve the best possible performance for more than just their own legal organization. Legal and operating control may call for separate reports and measures of performance, although preferably it should be clear how each relates to the other and how the two kinds of information "translate".

One difference is that in the imaginary organization (IO) we cannot actually expect the leader enterprise to have this kind of power over its partners. They may even consider that they belong to other—and possibly competing—imaginary systems. What can then be accomplished with the tools of management control?

The starting point is the imaginator and the leader enterprise. The imaginary concept determines the need for control. Unlike a mere network of companies, the IO has an intentional character: there is an investment at stake, with risks, and for a purpose.

Management control offers several interesting ways to influence what happens. It can provide structure and direction for the dialog which is an important element in the common effort to define a purpose. The language of management control has a powerful, although rather subtle, effect on the thinking and direction of various actors. It enables the imaginator to persuade by offering participation in the formulation of objectives, rather than by dictate or directive.

At the same time, there are risks. The most unambiguous accounting data may be much too precise. To discuss risks and profit-sharing with someone with whom we want to share our vision may be an utterly wrong approach.

Perhaps now the reader can understand why our material contains so few observations on what we have been discussing here. Consequently, our reasoning is largely theoretical. Does the establishment of information systems and regular dialog come at a later stage in the development of the imaginary organization?

INFORMATION FOR CONTROL

In the cases of the imaginary organizations which we have studied, the exchange of information is almost wholly informal. By contrast, the American literature on virtual organizations emphasizes that IT links and the presence of joint structural capital are at the very heart of the co-operative arrangement. The clearest examples are those of systems for reservations and similar purposes. Airline companies have tried to control IO-like networks of actors by establishing systems which, without ownership or other formal sources of power, nevertheless ensure that the travel agency or hotel acts in the interests of the airline. Here we also find a good example of an attempt to make a relationship more permanent by building up structural capital (a computerized system).

The cases which we have studied, however, are characterized by personal contacts. While these may be described in terms of measurements and dialogs, their essence is often just a repetition of the agreement among the parties in a network. However, to be considered as deliberately used instruments of control, the contacts should encompass more than an ordinary business agreement. For example, their purpose might be to make the involvees participants in the common enterprise in a larger sense, or to establish communication between different involvees. In Chapter 1 we have already discussed the importance of cohesive forces like these. But often structured communication is also necessary.

- *KalmarSalen.* "Information! That's what it's all about. You have to be extremely clear toward everyone involved to keep the network together and to deliver on your commitments. In an organization like KalmarSalen, you can't just talk and talk and let things develop as best they may" (this case is presented in detail in the Appendix).

Below we use as an illustration one of the possible IO forms discussed in Chapter 3. It should be viewed as an example. Other structures produce other patterns of contact.

Indicators

We expect communication primarily to cover the conditions for conducting operations, the instructions as to what should be done, and the description of what is to be achieved. By information for control, we thus mean not only instructions, but all information required for everyone to direct his/her action in the manner desired.

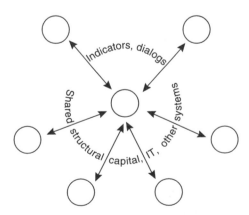

Figure 11.1   Information for control in the "spider web"

In traditional literature on control we find terms such as "task control", "program management", and "management by objectives". Under task control, controlling impulses and feedback refer to actions which are ordered and to their execution; under program management, they refer to rules for action; under management by objectives, they refer to what should be and has been accomplished. Companies often seek to use management by objectives whenever possible; both for the individual and for the organization, it is more encouraging to development and also more democratic.

All of these forms of management control may be present in the IO structure. Perhaps consistency with the IO concept would require that the more detailed forms of control be avoided. After all, it may be both difficult and inappropriate to issue orders to involvees who are not employees in a formal sense, although certain franchising arrangements do so to a high degree and may still fall into this category.

Thus, communication is primarily about the conditions under which the business is to be conducted, and about objectives. It may concern:

- *Information on customers.* The identity, characteristics, and previous purchases of customers are a natural base of useful data. An informal exchange of information, but one with a controlling effect, may take the form of a meeting at which the leaders of the participating companies discuss business and share their experience. A natural next step would be to formalize this exchange in the structural capital of a computerized customer data base for joint use. Access to such information has a value in serving as a basis for defining responsibility and roles in the co-operative arrangement:

  > The list of customers is available only to the conference bureau, not to partners. It is kept under lock and key. KalmarSalen seeks in every case to co-ordinate all operations involving the customer, both before and after an agreement has been reached.

- *Information on employees and involvees.* What talents do these people possess, and how can we develop them? Measurements proposed often seem too crude: development expenses per employee, etc. We mentioned some of them in Figure 10.3. Gradually we should arrive at better ways to take stock of competence, to document experience, and to measure commitment and loyalty. Fritzes and the People's Opera may not have formal files on writers and performing artists, but they need information on these people, including outside activities!

- *Information on products and methods.* Formulas, licenses, and the like indicate what involvees are entitled or obligated to do. These of course are also important elements of more temporary forms of collaborations. But in IOs they can be expected to serve as repositories of learning gained by all partners over time, constantly changing with new experience. By continuously collaborating people will learn how something should be done. The basic design, however, is often clearly controlled by the imaginator, who also checks to see that the work has been performed as intended. This statement should also be applicable to computerized ordering procedures, such as the systems of control which link up automobile companies with their suppliers.

- *Information on customer relationships.* The attitudes and opinions of customers are of course very important. Often, although not always, the leader enterprise has the direct contact with the customer. It is natural to encourage commitment by other involvees to the business as a whole: to interest them not only in fulfilling their obligations toward the leader enterprise but in appreciating the customer's reaction and in making suggestions for further improvement.

- *Costs/revenues.* Up to this point our discussion on ways to measure and describe what is going on has been about improving the odds of benefiting the customer by working together. In this respect there is a difference from management control in the traditional corporate environment, where the emphasis often is on cost control. Since the involvees in the IO belong to different legal entities, often with no common ownership, the need for (and the possibility of) sharing accounting information will reflect existing contracts. As a rule, these contracts, to which we will subsequently return, are ordinary business agreements, in which case the actual costs to each involvee concerns no other party. But in some joint venture projects, the efficiency of the respective parties is of interest to all of them; in such cases one might suggest developing an accounting system to provide relevant information for all involvees concerning the project as a whole. In this connection, it may be practical to use the same product designations, delivery terms, etc.

Dialogs

What forms exist for the exchange of the information we are discussing? We have implied that systems based on IT may be used, but the findings from our interviews indicate that meetings and telephone conversations play a very large part.

Normally in the exercise of management control, the most important dialogs are held in connection with budgeting and performance evaluation. At best the budget sets the stage for decentralized action during the coming year in furtherance of the business as a whole, without the necessity of continuous lateral contact. It may be difficult to find the proper balance between following the budget and adaptation to changing circumstances, but usually the budget provides the best guideline for local action consistent with the long-term objectives of the company.

Much of this reasoning is directly applicable to the imaginary organization. There, it is seldom realistic for all involvees to participate in formal budgeting, and even less so in the subsequent comparison of budgeted targets with actual performance. Neither do we advocate attempting to commit the parties to placing binding orders with each other far in advance. However, in the common interest of the business it might be desirable to consider what long-term orders might appropriately be placed, and who should bear the risks and costs? The leader enterprise may require an assurance of supply by involvees whose products/services are in great demand elsewhere, or who may even have a monopoly on services in a certain area. Depending on the balance of negotiating power, the leader enterprise may have to pay a price for the capacity which is held in reserve. But partner enterprises may also have to pay to participate, often by having certain computer systems or a particular competence.

In our case studies the dialogs seldom appear to be so formal that the parties share information on the basic assumptions underlying their budgets. However, joint meetings do tend to follow an annual rhythm, with kick-off conferences at the start of each season, for example.

Systems and IT support

As we have previously stated, the development of IT is regarded by many as an important factor contributing to the break-up of older, more self-sufficient companies. When communications are improved, it becomes easier to turn to others instead of keeping the necessary competence in-house:

- *KalmarSalen.* "KalmarSalen is critically dependent on modern information technology. You buy into a data bank on coming conferences. Your next step may be to enlarge the network connecting the conference bureau and the hotels."

In Chapter 9 we described how the imaginary organization may be regarded as a natural consequence of declining costs of co-ordination, or transaction costs. With improved communications, the cost of contact with the market decreases, and the scope of what it pays the company to do on its own becomes more limited. At the same time, many are increasingly doubtful as to whether a company can efficiently operate on its own in an area where it is not a specialist. Both factors encourage greater reliance on others—in the form of the imaginary organization, for example.

Structural capital

The concept of structural capital was introduced previously. The word "capital" denotes a long-term asset, not necessarily shown in the balance sheet but nevertheless owned and controlled by the company. While there is no generally accepted definition of structural capital, its use at Skandia illustrates a frequent interpretation (Figure 11.2). Included here are the systems and programs which we were just discussing. So are other documented procedures, data banks, and the like. One of their most important functions is to permit repeated application of successful ways of solving problems, and to reduce dependence on individuals who may decide to leave the organization. Solutions which have proved successful may also be reproduced by others. As far as possible, the formula for success should be made permanent in the form of structural capital. Otherwise success will depend on a few key people, and the company will be very vulnerable.

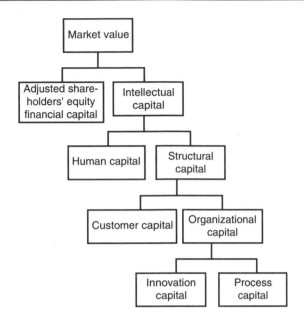

Figure 11.2 Structural capital and related concepts as used by Skandia (1996)

In some cases this task may be quite simple on a conceptual level, but very demanding in practice, including the procedures required, for example, in the case of customer contacts. Often, though, it can be difficult to give permanence to the formula for success; it may be what is termed "people-intensive", or in some other way impossible for those who use it to put into words. Even in cases like these, one normally sees considerable effort made to express what these people do in terms of a product, to describe their work step-by-step, and to invent a term for each step. At best, such efforts can increase the self-awareness of those concerned and improve the performance of their function.

In Chapter 9 we showed that if an imaginary organization is to thrive and grow, it will be necessary to articulate what makes it unique and to see that this uniqueness endures. For involvees to be true participants, they will need more than just intuitive knowledge. The knowledge required must be made accessible to a wider circle of people by means of systems and structural capital. The imaginator does not have the time to maintain personal contacts with all involvees. Therefore, the imaginary concept must be communicated in some other way, perhaps via media that will require an investment.

From the discussion above it should be apparent what kind of inter-company data may have to be developed for exercising management control in an IO. So far, we have found few instances in which this work has been done, perhaps because the IOs in our case studies have not reached a sufficiently advanced state, or because they are still too small.

- *Skandia.* In supplements to its annual reports for the last few years, Skandia AFS (see also Chapter 1) describes itself as an imaginary organization:

    By clarifying and refining its core processes, AFS acquires a competi-tive edge and the opportunity to be a market leader. With the help of partners considered to be "best-in-class" and the support of IT networks, this establishes the foundation of a federative organization that AFS

FINANCIAL FOCUS	1995	1994
Return on net asset value	20%	12.2%
Management operating result (MSEK)	247	115
Value added/employee (SEK 000s)	1.639	1.666
CUSTOMER FOCUS		
Number of contracts	87.836	59.089
Saving/contract (SEK 000s)	360	333
Surrender ratio	4.1%	4.0%
Points of sale	18.012	11.573
HUMAN FOCUS		
Number of employees (full time)	300	220
Number of managers	81	62
Of whom, women	28	13
Training expense/employee (SEK 000s)	2.5	9.8
Change in company's IT literacy	+2%	+7%
PROCESS FOCUS		
Number of contracts/employee	293	269
Adm. expense/gross premium	3.3%	2.9%
IT expense/adm. expense	13.1%	8.8%
Processing time, new contracts (days)	8	6
Processing time, changes (days)	3	13
RENEWAL 6 DEVELOPMENT FOCUS		
Premiums from nes launches	49.2%	11.1%
Increase in net premium	29.9%	17.8%
Development expense/adm. expense	10.1%	11.6%
Share of staff under 40 years	79%	72%

Figure 11.3 American Skandia's "Navigator" for 1995

calls "Specialists in Cooperation". This, in turn, incorporates the rapidly growing structural capital and substantial resources into AFS's network. It also makes AFS a so-called imaginary organization with a wealth of intangible resources that cannot be quantified by traditional metrics (Skandia, 1996, p. 14).

To measure these strategic resources, Skandia uses the concept of the *Balanced Scorecard* introduced by Kaplan and Norton (1996) and publishes information on various metrics as a "Skandia Navigator". A Skandia Navigator for American Skandia is shown in Figure 11.3. It should be kept in mind that these are metrics published for external use rather than those communicated between partners, but they may still give some idea of the variety of measures which should be considered for use.

EFFECTS AND REWARDS

The financial interaction between the leader enterprise and partner enterprises may also be described in another fashion. The management-control information which we have been discussing up to this point is of the kind which affects what happens. The next step is to divide the surplus which has been created. This process, too, calls for accounting information, but of another sort (Figure 11.4). As we have underscored, the benefits of the common enterprise should be multidimensional: for example, in the form of payments, participation in new business, contribution to learning, development, new contacts, and the pleasure and satisfaction of the work itself.

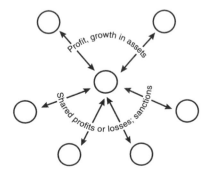

Figure 11.4 Effects and rewards

- *The Swedish Academy of Engineering Sciences (IVA).* IVA is a society of 375 leading figures in Swedish business and academia, with an emphasis on technical and economical science, and its practical application. There is also a larger advisory group of some 1300 people, and a core of some 60 employees. IVA observes and evaluates trends and acts as a lobbyist. Through its network it tries to encourage appropriate action. IVA acts as a respected interface to a large number of bodies outside business: government, universities, media, and the general public.

  But what are the benefits to the individuals who offer their time and enthusiasm? For many, undoubtedly it is the opportunity to influence something they perceive as important as citizens or in their professional role. Ericsson's CEO may see it as a chance to achieve "life-long learning for engineers", something of value also to Ericsson but difficult even for a large company to achieve on its own. To continue to realize this ambition, IVA must maintain not only a high profile but also a high level of credibility—although it is generally impossible to distinguish to what extent IVA's actions have influenced a government decision.

  Still, this arrangement can be regarded as an example of "sharing the rewards". The success of IVA has been due to its ability to influence political decisions. One may observe how politicians use arguments provided by IVA to support their positions, follow the advice of IVA, etc. IVA members (= involvees) feel that they have power, are in a position to influence subsequent events, and can establish a better basis for their own work.

Profits and the sharing of profit and loss

How profits and losses are to be shared is primarily governed by pre-existing agreements. Many leader enterprises simply purchase services, and if they become steady customers, they may be offered favorable prices. As for the sharing of risks, the imaginator knows his cost for each delivery, while the involvee bears the uncertainty as to how much business will be done. This arrangement may appear fair, but it does not provide much of an incentive for involvees to develop further.

We may find some guidance from industries which have long had an IO-like character. In publishing, royalties are the customary form of compensation for writers, while printers are paid for quantities delivered (in both cases there are, of course, industrial practices and competition). However, we also find fixed-price agreements with writers, as well as guaranteed remuneration. All these arrangements imply different ways of sharing risk, a determination which in the final analysis should reflect who is considered able to influence the overall outcome.

The basis for all commerce is that buyer and seller attribute different values to what is exchanged; otherwise, no transactions would take place. Similarly, the relationship between the actors must not be allowed to become a zero-sum game. All involvees must find that collaborating produces a benefit which exceeds the value of their input, at least in relation to their other options.

Consequently, the parties should preferably envisage several kinds of benefits from their agreement. This piece of advice is often given to negotiators: avoid a tug-of-war on a single issue, which frequently is how profits are to be shared; instead, try to find solutions in which both parties see that they stand to gain. Besides, "win–win solutions" should be possible if collaboration is truly justified and creates synergies.

Of course, the agreement will reflect the degree to which each party is indispensable, and thus their respective negotiating powers. This statement is particularly relevant when the parties must invest in know-how or equipment which will have value only if the imaginary organization is long-lasting and clearly successful (see Chapter 10 and Chi, 1994).

From the point of view of the imaginator, our advice would be to consider carefully what different involvees might want to obtain from collaboration. Often, and purely as a side-effect, the structure may create attractive opportunities which offer participants stimulation and potential for development.

Sanctions

The IO concept focuses on intraorganizational controls. You need to know about your partners in order to trust them, co-ordinate activities and assist them in developing their competence. The need is mutual, but for the leader company or the imaginator it is particularly urgent. The investment you make in your partners is often meaningful only if the co-operation continues. From time to time, you may raise the critical question of whether a change in partners would be beneficial, but the "switching costs" are often prohibitive.

We would then expect formal agreements on terms and duration of collaborations in IOs. However, in the cases which we studied, there were few examples of formal contracts. For that reason, it is also hard to find instances of sanctions to be imposed, for example, when one party opportunistically attempts to take advantage of the dependence of another. Naturally, an important question is how frequently such dependence is actually encountered. In fact, we have heard reports that the consequences of a break-up are often exaggerated. Of course, the duration of the arrangement, and the sincerity of the commitment to it, are significant factors.

Sanctions with more specific financial consequences are probably possible only when provided for in advance. However, informal, personal, or professional sanctions (ostracism) may be regarded as equally severe. In such cases, the aggrieved party must command a certain influence in the industry or in the media. Surely the situation is optimal when each party feels free to act in the pursuit of its own business and professional interests. Imbalance in the relative power of the imaginator and the involvees may arise from misjudgment at the outset, but also when one or more parties are limited in their freedom of action and thus vulnerable to exploitation by the others.

It should be re-emphasized that risks like these should be considered in advance. In reality they are probably difficult to regulate by legal means, in view of the importance, which we have noted, of a joint sense of commitment and will to develop further. Here we find one of the strongest reasons to keep the necessary competence in-house and not to become dependent on partners. Deceptive practices, prompted by self-interest, cannot be ruled out. We should remember, though, that what we want is often to harness the talent of some individual; even if we employ him, he can still act opportunistically.

Growth

A successful way to avoid disputes, or at least to postpone them, is to create a feeling among all concerned that the pie to be shared is continually growing.

Here too, of course, growth in several dimensions increases the likelihood that all involvees will be satisfied with their rewards. For example, even if an involvee only receives a modest share of growing profits, he may be allowed to participate in the more substantial and attractive part of the business, where he may find a better opportunity to improve his competence.

Rewards and information for management control

Information for management control should reflect and support the desired image of effect and reward. Even involvees under fixed-price contracts may be motivated to feel greater loyalty and to improve their performance if they are aware of the success achieved by the company. Measures of performance and dialogs should therefore reflect the image or vision which the company seeks to project. The concept of internal marketing has sometimes been used to show how employees' efficiency can be improved by influencing their image of their company. In the more tenuous structure of the imaginary organization, it may be vitally important to use every instance of contact with the involvees to develop the common vision and create a sense of participation.

- *KalmarSalen.* "Information, as when we repeat the message of the successes we have noted, is probably the best way to keep the whole business together."

CONTRACTS

The contracts (Figure 11.5) to which we refer concern for the most part the interaction among involvees and were previously discussed in Chapter 10. There we also suggested that the degree

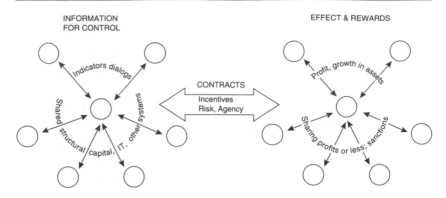

Figure 11.5 Contracts

of dependence and the measurability of results are important factors to consider when the contract is drafted.

Incentives

Incentives were previously discussed in Chapter 7. Relationships among involvees must not be allowed to become a zero-sum game. As in other negotiations, the benefits anticipated when the contract is reached should preferably be of several different kinds.

Risk

Risk is a consequence of our uncertainty about the future. Different risks arise from different conditions, and there are differences in the degree to which we can predict them and protect ourselves against them. The risks of collaboration should be identified and apportioned among the parties. If the imaginator decides not to do so, his decision should be a deliberate one.

In business finance, risk has a special meaning: what is the pattern of possible future events, or more precisely, what is the probability distribution of different outcomes, such as future profits? It is tempting to provide for a kind of insurance arrangement: a certain return is guaranteed, and the insurer bears the entire risk. When we take out an insurance policy, we pay a certain premium for the guarantee that there will be no additional cost to us in the form of other losses which may be greater. Some prefer to accept a deductible amount, thus bearing some of the risk themselves.

In our discussion here, we can apply a similar reasoning to the sharing of risk. There is uncertainty in all business. More complex products, in particular, provide examples of multiple risks. In the production of a movie, the cost of production and the interest of the viewing public may differ from what was expected. In collaboration, each risk should be borne by the party best able to foresee it and to affect its impact on the overall result. Purchases at a fixed price entail a different distribution of risk than purchases at current prices. However, to return to the case of the movie: if the production is to have genuine artistic value, and hopefully also attract audiences, perhaps meeting the budget should not be allowed to become an end in itself.

Agency Theory

In Chapter 10 we mentioned how contracts can put parties in a position of dependence, thus setting the stage for a kind of game in which one or both parties resort to opportunistic behavior—in other words, maneuver to obtain a tactical advantage.

The position of dependence arises because the parties are required to invest in assets, both material and non-material, which are of less value outside of the relationship. A company desiring to become one of SAAB's suppliers today would have to invest in computer links and quality control, and participate in consultations on development. As for SAAB, changing suppliers would be a protracted process. If the investment is extremely specific in the sense which we have been discussing, the investment should probably be kept within the company; otherwise there will be a potential for extortion. Furthermore, the investment should probably be financed to a larger extent than normal by the company's own funds. This discussion brings us to the question of how the companies are managed. Under the theory of agency, stock-holders and creditors are termed principals, and one seeks to identify the means by which they can exercise power over the company.

How does this reasoning relate to contracts in the imaginary organization? Primarily, it serves to emphasize that the parties should have foresight, and that the imaginator should truly have a unique contribution to make! While this point has been discussed in greater detail in Chapter 9, the conclusion to be drawn here is that simply taking the initiative is not enough. We have repeatedly indicated how the imaginator may risk being cheated, and we will return to this subject in Chapter 12.

For example, Teece (1992) relates how the British group EMI, which enjoyed a clear lead in computer tomography, lacked certain critical elements of the competence it needed to commercialize its know-how. For instance, it could not provide the support purchasers needed in operating and maintaining the equipment. As a result of the company's inability—in our terminology—to create the right form of imaginary organization, it completely lost a promising product. In Teece's opinion, EMI should have formed an alliance with Siemens. But it is not certain that this step would have helped. To persuade others to take the risk of investing in a relationship, a party must convince them that its contribution is essential in the long run. Otherwise they will first demand substantial compensation for their initial investment in development, and then later use their bargaining power to extract additional payment.

This reasoning underscores once again three critical factors for success: a clear, viable concept of business; contracts (formal or informal) which are multidimensional and can thus be interpreted as providing benefits to both parties; and some form of structural capital, under the imaginator's control, so that what has been developed will not be lost.

It is interesting to note how seldom the parties require exclusive dealing arrangements, to judge from our case studies. This observation may indicate that such arrangements are costly for both parties and that each sees a benefit in the potential for the other to develop its competence by serving outsiders. However, it is also conceivable that the imaginator underestimates its own risks—and the possibility of convincing the involvee of the benefits of closer co-operation.

SUMMARY

Under the heading of management control, we have covered a broad spectrum of issues concerning the use of formal, largely quantitative, measures for control purposes. We have discussed both internal and external management control, since what is external in a formal sense may in fact be an exercise of internal control.

Our reasoning has so far been hypothetical and forward-looking in the case studies available to us, we have seldom found examples of this form of control. We may be witnessing a particular stage in the development of the imaginary organization. However, some of the people with whom we have talked seem to believe that more tenuous ties, based on trust, are sufficient, and might even suffer from the formalization that could easily follow if quantitative reports and the like were introduced.

This observation stands in some contrast to the American literature on so called virtual organizations, in which the exchange of management-control information by IT is heavily emphasized. In addition, the more theoretical literature on transaction costs and the theory of agency underscores the need to restrain opportunistic behavior through formal agreements. Have we been studying the wrong companies? The basic model followed in this chapter can surely also be used to interpret the more informal contacts and relationships of dependence which we find in companies which do not see themselves using formalized reporting. And perhaps formalized reporting will emerge gradually with the growth of the imaginary organization.

The principal questions addressed in this chapter have been the following:

- *What information can be exchanged among the involvees in an IO structure?* Included in this category are joint data banks, planning conferences, communications networks, etc. Of particular interest are the attempts being made to establish structural capital which can give permanence to joint know-how.

- *How is success determined? Who receives what?* We noted that as in all negotiations zero-sum games should be avoided. This objective is often quite realistic, since benefits from participation can be found on many different levels.

- *What visible and invisible contracts exist?* It is important to have considered carefully the issues of incentives and sharing of risk, even if a decision has been made to avoid formal agreements. Incentives and arrangements for sharing risk should also be linked to management-control information and to measures of success.

It is interesting to note that many organizations now seem to make growing use of multidimensional descriptions of performance such as the Balanced Scorecard, to a certain degree downplaying the role of profit or return on investment as sole objectives in internal control. However, there are also proponents of reformed measures of profit, like Economic Value Added (EVA) (Stewart, 1991). For communication and contracts between partners in an IO, both types of measures should be considered. However, win–win solutions will be easier to achieve using multiple measures, a practice which also reflects the deeper and synergic character of the existing collaboration.

Up to this point we have been discussing questions relating to relatively short-run performance in the context of management control. But in the imaginary organization, investments and financing are also required. We will turn to this subject in the next chapter.

12
Financing and Ownership

In Chapter 11 we discussed the information required by the imaginary organization in order to monitor ongoing business. Building further means that some of the surplus created must be invested in development. Surplus here refers not only to financial gains, but also to other benefits of collaboration: new knowledge and improved processes, new contacts, and new data. These sometimes occur as a by-product of operations, but often they require conscious efforts to cultivate assets, know-how or material objects, which are only of value if the imaginary organization continues to operate. We mentioned that the parties must trust each other if the necessary investments are to take place; it may be most appropriate for different investments to be made by different partner enterprises.

We have already talked about structural capital, by which we have meant know-how incorporated in methods, computer programs, or data bases (see Figure 11.2.) It may also include a brand name, or some other way to preserve what otherwise exists only in the form of personal experience and contacts. To build up structural capital requires resources. Can the necessary investment be self-financed (if money is what is needed), or can it be made by the company's own efforts? What actors contribute, and how is the investment decision reached? What is needed to attract outside financing?

INVESTMENT AND FINANCING

Investing means giving up something today in order to get more tomorrow. In this sense much of what we do may be called investing, and our investment is far larger than what is shown on any balance sheet. Here, of course, we find the main reason for Skandia's analysis of its market value (see Figure 11.2). We invest in our own knowledge, we establish procedures, and we program computers. Industry expenditures on research and development and on marketing are estimated to be as great as its purchases of property, plant, and equipment.

These intangible investments are often the product of a company's own efforts. It is not easy to obtain financing for them from outside sources, since it is also difficult to show the "capital" thereby created, and the company cannot readily assert its ownership interest in this capital. What if key people leave? Financing is usually manifested in lower profits over the short run, since employees are devoting their time to furthering the company's long-term interests. One might contend that owners and creditors are indirectly providing the financing. They would probably think twice about their equity investment and the loans they had granted if they learned that the company had discontinued all its development projects!

In traditional companies, there are as a rule:

- *Investments in tangible assets*, normally with clear rights of ownership, accounted for as assets in the balance sheet, audited by independent accountants, and financed by the market.

- *Investments in intangible assets*, sometimes difficult to protect, with a value difficult to demonstrate, but considered necessary, and accounted for as current expenses.

The imaginary organization, too, must invest. We are not talking about the investments which each participating company may need to make on its own; for these, the reasoning just presented is applicable. Rather, we are referring to the need for involvees to invest money and effort in their joint enterprise. Several questions then arise:

- How is the initiative taken to make these investments?

- Who stands to gain, and who can be expected to put up the money?

- How is outside financing arranged when necessary?
- How are the risks assessed and shared?
- What information, internal and external, is needed about the investments?

Taking the initiative

It is reasonable to assume that the IO-leader usually takes the initiative in making an investment. In the imaginary organization, unlike other networks, investments are considered in relation to an imaginary concept. This perspective includes the opportunities, and the needs, for development.

Naturally, proposals may be made by an involvee, but these should be regarded more as bids submitted by suppliers. As we indicated previously, if an involvee decides to add to its know-how, or to acquire new computer equipment and the like in the hope of closer collaboration, it would be doing so as an individual company making a conventional investment.

The initiative taken by the IO-leader may be to create new systems of communication, or to train all involvees in their use. While the initiative is prompted by self-interest, it may often lead to "win–win" situations of the kind to which we referred in Chapters 10 and 11. In this case the involvees may agree to foot their portion of the bill. The various parties would then find mutual benefit in reinforcing their collaboration by making the joint investment. The only real difference is that the time frame is now longer.

However, some form of subsidy from the IO-leader's enterprise may well be requested, simply because the investment is perceived to benefit some parties more than others, or some involvees cannot afford to pay their share. We find instances in which partner enterprises are given training at no cost, or some of the financing is provided for new equipment. As a formal matter, the financing may be a loan, with a security interest in the equipment, or the leader enterprise may simply buy the equipment and locate it on the premises of a partner.

We now turn to another situation, in which the investment is primarily in the interest of the IO-leader. We have already discussed the use of structural capital to protect the core and make it permanent, and above all to eliminate the danger of dependence on involvees who possess virtually unique know-how. Building up structural capital can change the balance of power, so involvees have good reason to be wary. For example, if a new system of reservations can be operated by the customers themselves, travel agencies may no longer have any part to play in the arrangement.

The party who stands to gain foots the bill

Since the various involvees are independent companies, they decide for themselves whether to participate in an investment, and if so how much effort and money to put in. Although given the balance of power, it may be hard to refuse!

Expectations of future reward, based partly on formal or informal agreements, will of course determine how much a party is prepared to invest. As an example, let us consider joint product development in anticipation of business with some outside customer. Psychologically, it may be a rather big step for the IO-leader to purchase participation by the other parties instead of having each bear the cost of its own input. Even if the other parties should offer a favorable price as a gesture of friendship, the arrangement would still say something about the character of the co-operative arrangement, the sharing of risk, and the like.

Outside financing

The difficulty of financing intangible investments, even in conventional companies, has recently been the subject of considerable discussion. Yet there is much to indicate that precisely this kind of investment is becoming increasingly important in growth industries. Major corporations listed on stock markets in different countries often publish different profit figures under the rules of these countries. For instance, Ericsson's group profits are reported to be roughly 1 billion SEK larger under US-GAAP rules, as compared with Swedish ones. Most of this difference reflects capitalization of development expenses under the American rules, a practice not customary in Sweden. Some would like to introduce more of the "intellectual capital" (see Figure 11.2) into published balance sheets.

Actually, however, the discussion reflects larger issues of rights to intangible property, stockholder control, and sharing of risk. Perhaps it will be difficult to maintain the present corporate model of widely dispersed, impersonal ownership, with the requirement of financial statements and outside auditors, if business becomes a matter of investing, at risk, in specific know-how. Assessing the usefulness and credibility of the project will surely call for greater familiarity with the enterprise and its management.

If success is also dependent on the maintenance of peace in a network of involvees, outside investors may reasonably conclude that the risks are too great. The business risk—possibly considerable—of the venture itself is only one of them. Another is that if the investment does not pay off, the part of it devoted to building up the co-operative arrangement will have no residual value at all. And if the venture succeeds, how the reward will be shared is often far from clear. To review and audit what is happening, one would probably have to sit on the board of the leader enterprise—and even that position might not be enough!

Sharing risk

We have been discussing risks related to current business. For example, an involvee may have to put in more work than he gets paid for. When it comes to investments, the risks are much more substantial.

In our economy, it is normal for the risks assumed to be reflected in the balance sheet. The owners bear the risk, whether the outcome is positive or negative. The risk as measured by a probability distribution of different outcomes depends on the degree of equity financing. In the event of bankruptcy, creditors suffer only if there are not enough funds to pay the company's debts.

Of course the risk of an investment is borne primarily by the party who has paid for it. Sometimes the leader enterprise may assume all of the risk. But other involvees may also have to pay to participate in the joint endeavor, and sometimes—as in the case of franchising—even pay a fee to the leader enterprise. Can the risk be transferred to other financiers? The answer depends on what assets are accepted as security for loans, or in exchange for share capital.

Here there is a relationship to developments in the law of intangible property. But when we are talking about substantial investment in the accumulation of knowledge by individuals, probably they will have to assume most of the risk themselves. With the possible exception of the sporting world, it is hard to conceive of any ownership rights to the labor of human beings. Of course, one may imagine personal loans with clauses governing annual repayments, as with student loans, but in the case of more substantial investments, such an arrangement would resemble one of pure bondage.

A more attractive solution would be to make it easier for companies to set aside profits for investments which could not be reported as assets, and to let individual taxpayers equalize taxes over different years for similar purposes. Some of the risk would then be transferred to the public sector, which might be rewarded by greater tax receipts in the future—and hopefully also by favorable effects on employment and production.

Providing information

We will later return to the relationship between the imaginary organization (IO) and capital markets. At this point, we will examine how an investment proposal is presented in an IO.

Major investments usually require some form of project organization which transcends formal organizational boundaries. A considerable number of studies were done on such joint ventures in the 1980s.

It is difficult to describe the anticipated consequences of investments in research and development, marketing, training, and IT on the basis of customary investment calculations. Many of the parties concerned possess a portion of the relevant information, and it is important to ensure that their opinions and understanding enter into the process of evaluation. The criteria used here should contribute to a realistic assessment of how the investment might be used. There is often a risk that parties who would not bear the cost of the investment may make up long lists of possible uses, whereas the parties who would pay may be overly cautious, lest others get a free ride.

For an investment in structural capital and know-how, it is also important to find appropriate criteria for reporting on the current state of this resource and the degree to which it is utilized. We have thus returned to the subject of information for control, which was the point of departure for Chapter 11.

The business environment

In our previous discussion on investments, we brought up the subject of financial reporting for outside parties. To obtain the use of resources owned by outsiders, a conventional company must present an annual report which inspires confidence, as evidence of its value and justification of its credit rating. But since the imaginary organization does not exist in a formal sense, there are no financial statements for the business as a whole. The IO exists only in the mind of the IO-leader and of others who share his vision. Formal commitments can only be made separately by the individual companies which make up the IO.

The term "business environment" deserves some comment. The imaginary organization may be regarded as an open system, with boundaries that may be redefined at any time. However, there will be owners, creditors, business contacts, authorities, and other outside parties who seek to form an opinion on the companies in the IO. And for anyone intending to evaluate—perhaps even invest in, or do business with—the constituent companies, it may be important to understand the imaginary concept. Information on the companies, taken singly, may produce a very incomplete picture.

In several of our case studies, the parties appeared reluctant to formalize their collaboration. In those instances, there was very little to present to outsiders. Every company has a circle of reasonably faithful suppliers and customers—what is so different about this case?

Perhaps resources have been invested in the involvee companies in an attempt to commit them to a more permanent co-operative arrangement; if so, the reaction of outside parties may even be negative. Assets like computer networks may be worthless if the arrangement breaks up—in other words, if they may be termed IO-specific.

FINANCING AND OWNERSHIP

Our conclusion is that companies which require substantial outside financing to build up their IO structure will find it difficult to obtain the necessary funding through conventional loans or issues of stock. Owners with a better understanding of the business are needed, owners who are receptive to the imaginary concept. These parties, too, will probably want guarantees, including contracts with the involvees, which go beyond what the IO-leader would prefer. Owners who thus make it necessary to present the imaginary concept more clearly can serve a very useful function. The IO-leader who is strongly convinced of the validity of his vision may overestimate the willingness of involvees to contribute to its realization. Outside owners should also be committed to the concept, while at the same time keeping a certain distance in the knowledge that they are taking a risk. They may ask critical questions about what is being done to develop structural capital, to create a team spirit among involvees, etc.

Owners like these should be active members of the board of the leader enterprise. One model is for some of the involvees to become owners as well, but we are thinking primarily of situations which call for truly external financing. It would appear that the only way to obtain the necessary understanding of the business is by taking an active part in the work of the board of directors. While commitment as an owner will be based largely on intuitive judgments, these in turn require input data which can only be obtained from close contact with the business.

For the same reasons, investments should be largely self-financed, and there should be a high ratio of stockholders' equity to total assets. However, we should be careful about the meaning of these terms. The leader enterprise, in particular, may have to make substantial intangible investments which will not be shown in the balance sheet. The owners may encourage these efforts and accept limited profits during a build-up phase, so that the balance sheet will continue to reveal nothing about the investments. If an owner ventured to impute a value to them—and an owner who understood the business should be able to do so—the true ratio of stockholders' equity to total assets would be much higher even than the reported ratio, which might already be acceptable because of the low degree of indebtedness.

One way to reach a wider market is of course to offer for purchase and sale a "package" of stock in several of the collaborating companies, and for independent analysts to evaluate their prospects. However, it is difficult to determine the responsibility assumed by these analysts. For comparison, one may consider real-estate values in the 1980s, which were sometimes used in the annual reports of real-estate companies to justify valuation in excess of acquisition cost. The original ratio of stockholders' equity to total assets would then be artificially low; the "concealed" value of the real estate would increase stockholders' equity and total assets by an equal amount, thus improving the overall ratio (see Figure 12.1).

Generally accepted accounting principles do not permit us to report the value of intangible assets like programs and other structural capital in the balance sheet. It is sometimes maintained that such a prohibition acts as a deterrent to investments of this kind and creates difficulties for forward-looking companies; we will not discuss that issue further here. What we would point out, though, is that in the imaginary organization there is an additional difficulty—the concealed assets derive their value from collaboration among several legal entities. An asset can possess two kinds of value: its value as a potential capital gain if sold, and its utility value, which depends on the resourcefulness of the owner and on the context in which

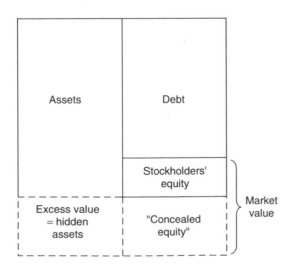

Figure 12.1 Concealed value in the balance sheet

the asset is used. Obviously, the utility value is the interesting one for the purposes of the present discussion. In our opinion, a proper determination of the utility value of an asset can generally be made only from within the IO, or perhaps from a position on the board of the leader enterprise. The answer depends on the difficulty of examining the context in which the asset is used. Will the co-operative arrangement endure? What will be the effect of the system of rewards? And what portion of the profit created will go to the leader enterprise?

Influence and control

We have stated that the owners should be close to the business, as active members of the board, for example. However, in a formal sense their control will remain limited, inasmuch as their ownership interest is normally only in the leader enterprise, not in the partner enterprises. In addition, their investment is often personal. Usually, the network will largely be a reflection of the imaginary concept; this concept, perhaps more than the company itself, may be the primary reason for having an ownership interest. Actually, this factor in itself is not sufficient to distinguish the IO from many other enterprises in the area of contracting.

In certain cases, we found that special circumstances characterized the function of the board of directors:

- *Folkopera.* To maintain popular support and perhaps also to carry more weight with official agencies that dispense subsidies for cultural activities, Folkopera (see also Chapter 5 and Appendix) has in practice separated the legal role of the board from a role more devoted to the development of the enterprise. As a formal matter, the separation is produced by having a foundation own the Folkopera corporation.

- *SCF.* The SCF program of continuing education (see also Chapter 6 and Appendix) is naturally of interest to the board of directors. However, since most of the customers are non-members of the SCF association, the board as representative of member interests probably regards the program as a business operation which the organization happens to conduct and which should produce a profit. In that situation the managing director finds it natural to seek the support of the chairman rather than that of other board members.

Financial accounting and valuation of the enterprise

As previously indicated, we are sceptical about explaining to an impersonal financial market what constitutes a particular imaginary organization, where it is headed, and what it is worth. This statement is especially true if we consider how to guarantee that this value can be preserved and protected. Using certain assumptions, we may of course calculate the total value added by the constituent enterprises and then compare it with what it would have been without collaboration. But as we have mentioned, success should often be multidimensional and long-term. To place so much importance on a single figure, representing an amount which no single party owns, just raises more questions appropriate to a zero-sum game.

Parties with a more personal interest in the operation—owners, business contacts, and perhaps official agencies as well—will of course need a description of some kind. The latter may follow the criteria used in internal reporting for the purpose of building self-confidence and a sense of participation. Examples might include various ways to measure the size of the business and the reaction of customers, general information on the division of functions in the network, and, in particular, explanatory notes on the core competence and structural capital. The criteria we have in mind resemble those which have been proposed for describing independent knowledge-intensive companies: number of customers possessing the relevant knowledge, profiles of each customer, ties to established customers, number of new customers, etc.

How much of this information to disclose is of course a question of tactics; the same is true of any efforts which may have been made to report the value of intangible assets. Whether we are correct in holding that much of this information should be disseminated to involvees to promote a team spirit, it is still hard to keep secret. Many imaginary concepts are difficult to copy in that they are based on trust, unarticulated knowledge, and relationships which have been built up over time. Information in these areas is less sensitive than, for example, the details of new IT solutions, where the competitive advantage consists in being the first to form a network and to obtain the commitment of involvees.

AN OVERVIEW

Figure 12.2 summarizes the basic model which we have built up step by step. The imaginary organization is symbolized by a pattern of partnership of the kind introduced in Chapter 1, with the IO-leader in the role of director, teacher, and coach. Of course the network may take some other form. The point is that someone needs to influence the pattern of action in the network in order for his business concept to work; this someone—usually without the power of ownership—must also play an active part in shaping the collaboration among the various partners, test and review whether it is appropriate to keep them in the network, and further develop his/her own imaginary concept according to its potential and the opportunities for new business.

For these requirements to be met, there must be *information for exercising control*. What does the IO-leader need to know about his partners, and vice versa? What formal collaboration exists: customer lists, ordering procedures, key ratios, measures of performance, planning methods?

Economics, including managerial economics, is about using resources efficiently. The critical issue of managerial economics is then one of *rewarding results*. How do you determine "performance": what are you supposed to achieve in the way of profits, growth, development of competence, etc? How do you share the benefits? What happens to a party which does not deliver on its promises?

Formal and informal *contracts* constitute the link between continual exchange of information and subsequent results. What do the actors consider to be their commitments within the IO structure? How are business risks shared? To what extent should these questions be answered in advance?

The upper part of our model (Figure 12.2) relates to on-going co-operation, which is often repetitive in nature. But to build further, it will be necessary to set aside some of what has been achieved for *investment* in development. We are talking about structural capital in the sense of the know-how embodied in methods, programs, etc.

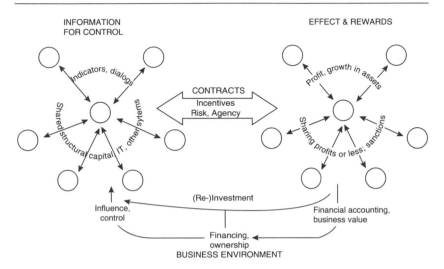

INFORMATION FOR CONTROL

EFFECT & REWARDS

CONTRACTS
Incentives
Risk, Agency

(Re-)Investment

Influence, control

Financial accounting, business value

Financing, ownership

BUSINESS ENVIRONMENT

Figure 12.2 Management control in the imaginary organization

This reasoning is symbolized by the lower link in the Figure, from results and rewards back to information for control.

However, internal resources will not suffice for major investments. Support and financing from the business environment *outside* the IO will also be required. If the IO is to obtain these resources, it must provide financial accounting with information that can convince outside parties of the value of the business. How can the IO report assets which are largely intangible? What arrangements should be made concerning ownership and the exercise of influence and control by the owners? One way, among others, is to ensure them that the systems of management-control information, of contracts, and of results and rewards are reliable and provide the foundation for the information presented in the financial accounting, etc.

SUMMARY

In this chapter we have discussed the following questions:

- *How are investment decisions made, and who provides the neces-sary resources?* Usually the IO-leader can be expected to take the initiative. Often the investment takes the form of efforts on the part of the IO-leader rather than costly purchases from outside. Therefore, investments are favored by an arrangement in which each party provides its own contribution.

- *How does the owner exercise control? What will the bank want to know?* Probably ownership will not be limited to the usual anonymous arrangement of financial markets, but will permit close scrutiny of the business. Measuring the value of the imaginary organization or of the leader enterprise is of less interest than portraying the imaginary concept.

13
Leadership—More Managing by Fewer Managers

NEW ROLES FOR MANAGERS

In imaginary organizations many of the involvees will manage their own partner relationships. Each involvee makes decisions in his own sphere and together with people in other areas on which his own is dependent and with which it interacts. Especially in small IOs, as some of those in our study are, there are many individuals who must be their own bosses, managing themselves and their businesses.

Being your own boss

Everyone in an imaginary organization spends considerable time influencing and being influenced by others.

Individuals and groups are expected to perform much of the day-to-day management which in a conventional company would be the responsibility of a manager in the formal sense: e.g. division of labor, spreading information, resolution of conflict. They must exercise autonomy, self-discipline, and the responsibility for the development of their own competence.

An important skill is the ability to establish and maintain a network of contacts. Networks are built up and used to define, redefine, and perform what is to be done. They are governed through informal contacts on the basis of personal preferences, the competence of various people, and the problems which are currently acute.

To function in a network, a person must be able to co-operate with others in the network. He/she will have to interface with many different functions, business units, customers, etc.—not only responding to the needs of the task but also adapting to different organizational cultures. Trust in the competence of others is essential.

- *SCF.* "You will be successful if you are highly motivated yourself, and if you can motivate others—both employees and involvees. Also if you have a large network and can maintain it through discussions which produce and evaluate exciting ideas. The involvees are the key; you have to find out what they think and what they are able to do."

From manager to spider in the web

The work of the few managers in an imaginary organization differs from that of their counterparts in hierarchical organizations. In the latter, we find direct management and a focus on the resolution of acute problems; in the IO, by contrast, we find performance evaluation, resolution of intergroup conflict, formulation of objectives, and development of competence. Managers in an imaginary organization also "serve" a much larger number of persons.

In an imaginary organization managers serve networks as well; in other words, they function in networks and groups rather than managing individuals. The members of these networks and groups are expected, in turn, to manage themselves. The responsibility of the actual manager is to see that individuals and groups perform as agreed, and to set clear limits in regard to other groups and outside interests.

- *Folkopera.* "All of the three leaders are active in representing the theater. They also try to take turns in being the one who receives the guests of a particular sponsoring company, etc.

  The network of contacts is important. Many artists leave Folkopera after a particular production, perform somewhere else, and come back later. That is all right as long as you don't lose touch with them. As the years have gone by, a store of know-how on dealing with different problems has been built up at the core of

Folkopera, and personal contacts with business and the public sector have been extended and enhanced.

Business contacts are well documented. Notes are also taken on performers but are supplemented by recollection: 'She auditioned three years ago. Wouldn't she fit the role now''

Maintaining competence is another central duty of managers in an imaginary organization. Considerable time is spent on the development of competence, including core competence. Various methods are used—facilitating contact between different parts of the IO so that each may get to know and learn from the other, establishing networks of know-how, appointing people to see that know-how is spread throughout the IO.

Co-operation and mutual trust are key words. They connote management by process rather than management by function. The former method is very demanding and calls for a high degree of flexibility in management processes and systems. It may be uncomfortable for managers accustomed to hierarchical organizations, who feel that they are losing control.

New positions

Management in IOs is based on knowledge rather than power. The difference between managing and doing the work is diminishing in that information is available to everyone and that control over the work is linked to competence. The channels of communication are direct.

As the leader enterprise grows, it begins to need various supporting functions. Table 13.1 presents what might be some supporting functions of imaginary organizations.

From executive group to service group

In an imaginary organization, strategic issues are not the exclusive province of top management. Every independent operating unit will have these issues on its agenda if we define strategy as the approach taken to the development of the unit's business.

Table 13.1 New positions

Hierarchical organizations	Imaginary organizations
Controller	Controller of competence
Director of finance	Director of intellectual capital
Personnel director	Director of networks
Director of logistics	Director of creativity
Purchasing director	Director of motivation
Director of infrastructure	Director of mental frames
M/A (mergers and acquisitions) expert	M/V (meaning and visions) expert
Manager of investor relations	Manager of partner relations
Investment trust officer	Personal trust officer
R&D manager	Director of unlearning
Payroll office	Office of rewards and incentives

At Skandia AFS there is a director of human resources with the title "Director of Intellectual Capital".

In an imaginary organization, there are many who must perform their own strategic analyses and act on the conclusions reached. A study (Bartlett & Ghoshal, 1994) of management in successful new companies shows that the new executives focus their effort on:

- Formulating an appealing mission for the business rather than developing and following a clear strategy.

- Focusing on management processes rather than establishing formal structures.

- Developing the competence and perspective of personnel rather than controlling their work.

The above is applicable to the imaginary organization. The mission of management is to facilitate the identification of problems rather than to present solutions. The transition is difficult for many who are accustomed to working in hierarchical organizations. It appears that executives as well as other employees of these conventional companies continue to believe in the myth that strategic development is something done by top management.

Innovation seldom begins with top management. It is picked up and propelled forward from the most unexpected quarters. Not that top management typically fails to see changes that call for action. Strategic management consists in knowing when the time is right to unleash the forces of innovation and to break away from the established pattern. Whether the process can then be controlled is a good question. There are always numerous unseen and untested business opportunities which would not require massive resources to exploit.

The art of strategic management is to be able to innovate while maintaining stability. The dynamic element of management lies in choosing the focus, organizational form, and technology of the business, the static element in achieving operational efficiency through stability, a minimum of disruption, and quality performance.

THE FUNCTIONS OF MANAGEMENT

Imaginary organizations have the same management functions as other organizations. Management is about architecture, productivity, and efficiency as well as attraction (Arbnor et al, 1993). The role of the leader enterprise is to build an architecture for a common vision, to develop the necessary arrangements for assuring the development of competence, for creating value for customers, etc., and to establish relationships on the basis of mutual attraction (Table 13.2). These three functions of management—architecture, productivity, and attraction—vary in importance during different phases in the development of the business of an imaginary organization (Table 13.3).

At the outset there is usually a clearly identifiable architect or core of architects.

- *Folkoperan.* At Folkoperan, the Managing Director has remained a singer and thus kept in touch with the artistic side of the operation. He has thereby found it easier to gain the confidence of other artists. The group has thus been spared the confrontation so often encountered in the theater between artistic ambition oblivious to financial limitations, and administrators with no sense of artistic value.

Many of the involvees in imaginary organizations must be able by themselves to make decisions affecting their own efficiency and productivity. They are their own theatrical directors. For the IO to work, the involvees must also be capable of establishing good relationships and networks. Otherwise the IO will fall apart.

Table 13.2   Management functions

Architecture	Productivity	Attraction
Create a common vision	Develop and organize the common structure required for productivity, efficiency and motivation	Create a culture which generates synergies
Identify and express the concepts of business		Make use of and transmit expectations and opportunities from and between different persons and groups within and outside the IO-involvees, customers, and stake-holders
Define the distribution of functions and competence among the leader enterprise and other involvees		
Concept of business	**Concept of work** **Concept of human resources**	**Concept of attraction**

The most critical management function is to cultivate the attractiveness of the imaginary organization. Management must create expectations and see that they are fulfilled, or perceived to be fulfilled. The IO-leader must set up the right conditions for all involvees to do a good job. These conditions include contacts, awareness of the business as a whole and where it is going, and support in development of competence.

Architect

The management of an imaginary organization must create and develop its architecture. Among the foundations of the edifice are vision, concept of business, and strategy for learning. The vision and the concept of business serve as guidelines for everyone so that each can do the right things in the right way—in other words, be both productive and efficient.

- *Skandia AFS.* Some of Skandia AFS's core values are: *Philosophy*: We create financial tools for continued Quality of Life.

Table 13.3 Different functions of management in different phases of an imaginary organization

Management functions	Different phases				
	Emergence	Start	Growth	Maturity	Renovation/ discontinuation
Architecture Architect	Create a vision and a concept of business	Build up the structure of the business	Refine the structure Refine the concept of the business	Renew the concept of business and the structure	Reuse old resources in new constellations
Productivity Theatrical Director	Create a concept of work (including forms of communication and control) and a concept of human resources	Oversee all the work	More of the work is taken over by employees and involvees Build up necessary joint systems	Give advice	Create a new concept of work/of human resources
Attraction Creator of expectations	Communicate opportunities	Communicate expectations and values	Show how expectations are to be met Affirm values	Attract new involvees	Create new expectations

Mission: We are dedicated to improve personal financial well-being by offering long-term savings solutions, in a chaotic and ever-changing world.

Intellectual capital: We will create a competitive edge by focusing on intellectual capital.

Economics: We will search for cost effectiveness through innovative and non-conventional solutions and building on experience gained from others.

Dynamics: Your actions and interactions focus on time and quality and create the success of Skandia AFS.

The concept of business, or "mission", must be developed, spread, and convincingly presented to all involvees in the business—not only to employees. It must find support and confirmation. This work requires symbols, spokesmen, and leaders.

The architect must also establish conditions favorable to learning. He/she must design ways of doing the work and of exercising leadership which provide contact with customers, develop a sense of the business as a whole, and bring out the common vision.

In conventional companies management is supposed to show:

- That it has innovative and strategic capability.
- That its efforts have led to measurable results, whether these be improved profits, discontinuation of a business, or cost-cutting for survival.

In a business characterized by networks, accessible information, and division of labor according to competence, the criteria will probably be different. It will be important to:

- Have access to a large and functioning network.
- Enjoy working with others.
- Add value by creating and fulfilling expectations in different parts of the organization and its network.

The competence of the architect in an imaginary organization is partly a matter of knowledge and experience gained from both outside and inside the imaginary organization. He will need to be skilled in strategy formulation and in negotiation. An extensive network will be necessary, as of course will be the drive to make a difference and to create something of lasting value.

The role of the architect is most pronounced when the imaginary organization is created. Then it is usually associated with a single person. As the organization grows, the role is gradually assumed by several others. Many people have an impact on the architecture of the IO. The founder may in fact jeopardize its growth by spreading the myth that strategic development is the sole province of management.

Theatrical director

The business must have a "theatrical director". There must be a concept of the work to be performed and a concept of the role of human resources. These concepts of the work to be performed determine how the various parts of an imaginary organization should interact, exchange information, divide the work, etc. The concept is reinforced by the way the work is done and by existing structures. It provides a guideline which is usually quite general rather than detailed. The concept of human resources indicates the kind of people who are to become involvees and employees.

The imaginary organization is based on the assumption that maintenance and improvement of productivity and efficiency are largely the responsibility of the partners and involvees themselves. Each is accountable for the development of his own productivity and for keeping it in line with that of others. The role of the leader enterprise is to supervise, to give advice, and to take the initiative in establishing the systems necessary to ensure that adequate attention will be paid to such areas as development of competence, customer value, and exchange of information.

The primary mission of management is to see to the maintenance and development of necessary competence. There are many different ways of maintaining competence, such as facilitating the exchange of ideas, promoting mobility among different parts of the IO, establishing banks of know-how, and creating networks for its exchange.

- *Skandia AFS.* "At Skandia AFS we try hard to encourage a spirit of competition among the different parts of the organization, but it is also important to see that necessary competence is transferred from one unit to another" (Managing Director, Skandia).

The leader or the leaders of the IO must keep in touch with what is happening and know whether the business is developing along the lines which have been agreed upon and set forth. This controlling function is performed by evaluating results according to agreed criteria, by mediating in conflicts between various parts of the organization, and by observing signals from customers. More specifically, this function entails:

- Seeing that what has been decided on gets done.
- Evaluating the constantly occurring variances, serious or not so serious, between plans and results.
- Initiating analyses, projects, and other studies to find ways to eliminate recurring problems.
- Maintaining the commitment of employees and other involvees and their interest in developing themselves and their work.

The competence of the theatrical director is partly a matter of knowledge and experience in business administration and management. He/she must be capable of influencing others and winning their support, and of preparing an agenda of the right issues. Critically important to this role is a willingness to serve others and a positive attitude toward them. The theatrical director must be skilled at working with little fact and great feeling.

- *SCF.* "Qualities of the IO-leader might include the attitude that we always have the resources, that things can always be arranged. He/she does not like budgets. Can live with uncertainty and constant change. Understands that an ambition to build empires has no place in the IO. Has no ambition to be the house hero, is not afraid to lose face, and can live with the idea that the balance sheet will never be anything to boast about. Realizes that the best way to gain power and influence is by being better informed."

Creator of expectations

Relationships within the imaginary organization and with its business environment are the focus of the third critical management function. All stakeholders must receive what they have expected.

- *Skandia AFS.* "Skandia AFS is the leader in a network of leaders of other networks." (Managing Director, Skandia).

IO-leaders must make the constellation attractive. It must identify and match up the expectations of different groups, customers, and stakeholders both within and outside the IO. It must serve a purpose larger than just paying adequate compensation to involvees and employees, furnishing customers with a functionally appropriate product or service, contributing to economic growth, etc. More and more, the function of management is to create value in the form of meaning, quality of life, and responsibility.

- *IMIT.* "Management spends a lot of time establishing and maintaining relationships. Personal contacts may mean the difference between success and failure."

In various ways, this function entails explaining and underscoring the values, culture, and role of the imaginary organization. The purpose is to maintain a balance among different stakeholders in the business. It is important to create appropriate expectations (Ljung, 1992).

When the imaginary organization is established, the creation of expectations is the principal function of the founder himself. As the business grows, other creators of expectations emerge in various parts of the IO. In conveying the message about how different elements of the business are interrelated, these people play a key part in the emergence of relationships and a common culture. They help employees, other involvees, customers, etc. to see the whole picture rather than just certain aspects, thus providing a meaningful context in which others can form opinions and take action.

The role of IO-management is to see that relationships and the flow of knowledge remain open and develop further, to create expectations and to show how they can be met. The job calls for no small measure of diplomacy, in that it involves reconciling different interests and seeing that all parties stand to gain.

Creators of expectations possess a competence which includes knowledge in diverse areas and an ability to establish networks. These managers must also be able to help employees and others to understand and use the system. Like the theatrical director, the

Table 13.4 Different kinds of management competence in different phases of an imaginary organization (influenced by Bengt Johannisson's (1992) studies of ways in which entrepreneurs learn)

Kinds of competence	Different phases				
	Emergence	Start	Growth	Maturity	Renovation/discontinuation
Knowledge, Skills, Experience	Creativity	Marketing	Contacts and trust / Business administration	Commitment and motivation	Creativity
Networks	Networks to form concepts	Networks to create expectations	Networks for reinforcement	Networks to renew concepts	Networks to create expectations
Values	Wants to create something	Want to create something / Likes to establish and have relationships	Wants to create something / Likes to establish and have relationships	Likes to establish and have relationships / Wants control over own life	Wants to create something

creator of expectations must have a positive attitude toward others; like the architect, he/she must have the urge to create something.

Management competence in different phases of the imaginary organization

Architect, theatrical director, and creator of expectations—these IO functions are shared by a number of people. Usually the IO-leader, or a small core around him/her, assumes the roles of architect and creator of expectations, whereas many play the part of theatrical director. The tools of the theatrical director are the agenda and a knowledge of business management. The architect and the creator of expectations must rely totally on their competence in perceiving business opportunities and in establishing networks.

The importance and content of these different kinds of competence vary over the life of the imaginary organization (Table 13.4).

SERVANTS RATHER THAN LEADERS

An imaginary organization is formed around a core of ideas, competence, and needs, and it cannot develop unless the challenge of its needs and opportunities has broad appeal. For many are needed who are willing and able to manage themselves and to help others develop their competence and effectiveness. This statement is often an article of faith in imaginary organizations. The role of the leader or of the leaders in an IO is to identify and articulate needs. These people represent the culture and effectiveness desired; they are the driving force of an IO.

- *The Värmdö Office of Cultural Affairs.* "The Office has learned to work through others and without fear of losing face, to be sensitive to others and non-bureaucratic. Others are free to take the credit."
- *IMIT.* IMIT has established long-term personal relationships with key people in a number of industries. These on-going contacts generate a stream of ideas and suggestions about problems that need research. The program managers at IMIT have a role similar to that of a movie producer. They are to

see that the script—the application for research funding—is submitted and evaluated. They are to arrange financing. They are to select actors—researchers and other personnel. They are to manage negotiations and conclude them with a contract. They are to make sure that the filming (the research) is completed on time and within a budget. Finally, they are to see that the production under their responsibility reaches a large audience.

Servant leadership

People who are attracted to imaginary organizations value independence in their work. They want to know and understand what is happening. Decisions from above are not accepted until they are understood and the alternatives have been presented. These people want to contribute their competence and do not like to be overlooked. It is important for them to know how their competence can be used and developed further.

The function of IO-management is to set goals and evaluate performance on the basis thereof, but even more, it is to create conditions favorable to learning. The role of management is to help others learn from their experience, to acquire the capacity to respond to change, to promote innovation, and to manage and develop themselves.

- *IMIT.*   IMIT tries to avoid is being regarded as a parasite with little to contribute—there would then be a danger that researchers and institutions would run their projects on their own. One antidote is an efficient operation. It is also important to have strong program managers who "own" the customer relationship and access to sources of financing for the projects.

For this purpose people are needed who are good at listening to those they want to influence, and who can help them to do a good job, can maneuver in the IO, and can encourage them in their development. Thus, the focus is neither on leadership nor on being a manager, but on servant leadership (Greenleaf, 1977).

The concept of servant leadership has to do with helping employees and other involvees to learn from change, to innovate, to control, and to develop personally and professionally. The spirit of servant leadership implies being a listener, focusing on what one has to do, having a sense of strategy, seeking to understand, being capable of empathy, and being able to work together with others. You start with a natural desire to serve others; you end up wanting to lead (Greenleaf, 1977).

Involvee leadership

The involvees' own leadership is just as important to the successful IO as is servant leadership. Personnel (both employees and other involvees) must assume responsibility for their own development while also contributing to the learning of colleagues and other involvees. Everyone in an IO must learn to act without the support of a hierarchy and without access to a staff of experts. Their success will depend instead on how much they can contribute to the success of their colleagues and other involvees in various ways: by selecting the right people to work with, by working with them in the right way, by introducing the right people to each other, and by providing inspiration and acceptance for new ideas and knowledge.

IO-involvees must be generous with their knowledge, assume the responsibility for their own learning, and help their colleagues to learn. In so doing, they reinforce their own competence and keep it in demand. The dialog produces an exchange of knowledge, thus adding to the competence of the parties. Everyone must assume a responsibility for learning that will benefit the entire business.

Most people learn best when they force themselves to transcend their own boundaries. It is important that the IO encourage and make it easier for employees and other involvees to take on new assignments, to try new approaches and ways of working.

Innovation often arises when people interact—within or outside of the enterprise. Learning is typically accompanied by extensive collaboration across formal boundaries. Perhaps customers are the most underestimated source of new knowledge. Successful IOs involve their customers in the development of their knowledge.

The spirit of involvee leadership may be characterized by:

- *Generosity with knowledge.* Knowledge is one of the few assets which we still have even after we have given it away. Still, many people keep a lid on their knowledge to make sure that it will remain in demand. The opposite attitude is more likely to bring success. By being generous with knowledge, by assuming responsibility for their own learning and helping colleagues to learn, people are more likely to receive new knowledge in return. Thus, the dialog produces an exchange of knowledge which in turn adds to competence.

- *Readiness to allow and admit mistakes.* "Trial and error" is a recognized method for acquiring new knowledge and skills. Still, far too seldom are we given the opportunity to learn from others' mistakes so that we can avoid them ourselves. In an open culture, one conducive to learning, each person assumes a responsibility for the learning of others. There, it is natural to talk about your failures as well as your successes; together, you and your colleagues consider what has happened and draw conclusions for the future.

- *Courage to accept new challenges.* As previously stated, most people learn best when they force themselves to surpass their limits. It is important to take advantage of every opportunity to receive new assignments, to try new approaches and methods of working.

- *Assuming responsibility for your own learning.* Being a responsible employee or involvee also means knowing yourself, keeping track of what works and what does not, taking the initiative in designing your own plan for personal and professional development, and then implementing that plan.

- *Putting the job ahead of short-term self-interest.* Many people focus on short-term self-interest, to the detriment of their employability later on. But if they devote their energy to the relationship, the contract, between employer and employee, among colleagues in a work group, etc., then their learning will also be properly focused. It should be added that developing the management skills of managers is not enough. The management skills of other personnel must be developed as well.

SUMMARY

An imaginary organization requires the same management functions as do other goal-oriented activities conducted in concert. Management is about vision and structure, efficiency and productivity, attraction and relationships. The main difference is that in an IO these functions are shared by a number of people in several companies outside the leader company. Much management is done by involvees.

The most critical element of management competence is the ability to establish and maintain networks.

The IO is totally dependent on involvees who by their own efforts develop themselves, their work, and their colleagues.

The predominant style of management will then be neither leadership, nor management in the narrow sense, but one characterized by a servant leadership and involvees' own leadership. The latter two concepts focus on the ability to learn from change, to innovate, to exert control, and to develop oneself and others.

Good leadership is impossible without good management. Management provides the structures and systems required to facilitate and reinforce learning. A servant leadership is of no use without a leadership from the involvees themselves.

14

Creation, Renovation, and Extension—A Summary

At different times, and most recently in the 1960s and 1970s, many have believed that the planned economy and hierarchical management would be more successful than the market economy with its many small separate companies, the cost of co-ordinating their operations, and the difficulty of inducing them to make long-term investments; people then placed a growing faith in policies of industrial localization and state ownership. The planned economy has also been regarded as the solution to many problems of the Third World. But especially in recent years, the belief in the planned economy has been repeatedly shaken in its foundations. At the same time, with the emergence of modern information technology, a new way has opened up to connect and co-ordinate "islands of enterprise". In a number of cases, transaction costs have declined so sharply that new forms of organization have become possible.

A PERSPECTIVE WHICH LEADS US FORWARD

An imaginary organization represents an attempt at an intermediate form of doing business, a kind of market contract with certain long-term features and in some respects a systematic approach to the relationships between the parties. While the involvees clustered around the leader enterprise are independent and do their business on that basis, in certain selected respects they have chosen to participate in a game directed by the IO-leader. The development of competence, the focus of investment, and other major factors bearing on the direction taken by the business, are influenced by the IO-leader's vision of the future. Certainly subcontractors have always had to adapt to the long-term planning of a major customer. But here the involvee companies in some ways may act as if they belonged to a large corporate group; they may co-ordinate their systems of information, participate in the same training programs, and in dealing with certain customers represent the imaginary organization in name and appearance.

In respects critical to the realization of the imaginary concept, the IO-leader retains a power normally possessed by the chief executive of a hierarchical corporate group, whereas in other respects the field is left fully open to market forces. The principal function of the IO-leader is to choose partners and to design a common structure so that the competence and efficiency of the combined enterprise is optimal for the business. The sphere of joint activity usually includes the approach taken toward the customer, investment in competence by the involvees, and the use of joint infrastructure—primarily IT-assisted—for co-ordination and the transfer of information.

There is a clear parallel between this balance of central control and independence, and the discussion on *subsidiarity* in the European Union (EU). There, at least in theory, we find a federation of nations which have voluntarily ceded certain decision-making powers to common, democratically elected bodies. An imaginary organization is similar to such a federation in that the involvees have freely chosen to accept the IO-leader's vision and the consequences thereof. The degree of decentralization will then be determined primarily by relative advantage with respect to competence and by possible gains from synergy. However, the imaginary organization is held together by the concept of a common business, and not—as in the EU—by political ground rules, elections, and representation.

Throughout this book, we have emphasized that the imaginary organization should primarily be regarded as a fruitful *perspective*—new to many—on business development. The perspective may serve as a blueprint for creating a new business, or as a basis for renovating an existing company. In both cases it is a matter of developing appropriate *forms for creative organization*. And in both cases the organization will transcend existing boundaries and pose a challenge to the traditional concepts of "company", "managerial economics", "accounting", and "leadership", as the focus of perception and as subjects of regulation.

The IO perspective can form the basis of an overall approach to co-ordinating various resources to meet customer needs in a way that increases the value obtained from the resources used. The enterprise can grow without becoming larger. It can create more while using less through organizing its business environment as well as itself, utilizing the resources of others, and making synergy possible. Thus, the limitations of the IO-leader's organization and its stockholders' equity become less constraining. Capital, commitment, and—above all—various sources of competence and know-how can be provided by others so that the concept of business can be realized. In such a system, the critical factors for success can be expressed in terms of ideas such as customer orientation, value creation, involvement, common vision, co-ordination of core competence, pursuit of quality, and putting trust, knowledge, and capital to good use.

In an interesting study by INSEAD (1993), 108 major European manufacturers of various mechanical-engineering products were examined in regard to their development strategy and profit performance during the period 1989–91. The study shows clearly that total quality management (TQM) was the predominant development strategy at the time and that this deliberate effort to improve quality paid off in more rapid inventory turnover, greater customer satisfaction, shorter production times, and more accurate delivery. However, the study also shows that this focus on TQM had only a very marginal effect on profitability and market share. Effective efforts at TQM appear to have been a prerequisite for simply keeping up with the competition, and most of the leading companies became good at it; in other words, it was a necessary but not sufficient condition for growth and success. In a comment on the INSEAD study, Arnoud de Meyer (1993), Associate Dean at INSEAD, states that for companies seeking to enlarge their market and raise their profits, it will probably not suffice to pursue even the most admirably executed trim-down strategy within existing limits. They must also undertake *organizational innovation* if they are to stand out from the crowd. As de Meyer interprets the results of the study, some of the companies reviewed are now clearly preparing for the next step: the virtual, boundary-transcending factory which more purposefully co-ordinates its own resources and those of others for optimal utilization of core competence, synergy, and sharing of knowledge.

Such a trend is quite consistent with our view. Using an IO perspective will make it easier to see new opportunities to remove extraneous elements from one's own business, and to combine it with the resources of others so that a new situation arises, primarily from an organizational innovation which has put the business a step ahead of its competitors. Someone with a new concept of business can create the operation right from the start using IO blueprints. In this way, resource constraints can be eliminated, and more rapid growth can be made possible. Probably, an IO perspective will also permit a more radical approach to learning (one entailing structural change) of the kind which Chris Argyris, management consultant and researcher on organizational learning at Harvard, terms "double-loop learning" (Argyris & Schön, 1978).

INFORMATION TECHNOLOGY—IMPORTANT, BUT NOT ALWAYS A PREREQUISITE

In current American debate, modern information technology is usually depicted as a prerequisite for the new virtual companies. The notion of virtual companies brings to mind computer technology, with terms like virtual memory and virtual reality. One reason why we have chosen the designation "imaginary organizations" is to avoid automatically being associated with IT. But of course imaginary organizations are in large measure creations of our time: the new forms of business for the information society. We have also shown how co-ordinated information systems, customer data bases, etc. are perhaps the most important resource in many of the companies in our case studies. And we have touched on the more general trend toward replacing the hierarchical organizational design of the industrial society by horizontal co-ordination, and by networks at points where IT lowers transaction costs so much that new forms of organization become feasible.

Further, we have underscored the enormous importance of structural capital in the imaginary organization. And information technology is becoming an increasingly common example of such structural capital. One application is in the communication between leader and partner enterprises. Another is in programs made available to partners by the leader enterprise to facilitate the transfer of information needed throughout the imaginary organization, guarantee a certain standard of quality, ensure uniformity with regard to customer service, etc.

However, many of the companies in our case studies have not developed very far along such lines. In small imaginary organizations the number of contacts is limited. In the initial phase, building a network probably requires more person-to-person contact than IT. Still, we believe that the development of IT structures will have a growing impact on the future of the imaginary organization; IT permits efficient selective co-operation among its various parts. With communications technology, co-operation is relatively unconstrained by time and place. Rapid changes are taking place in the international division of labor. Companies seeking to cultivate their own globally effective competence will surely have to keep pace with developments in IT. In addition, collaboration with different actors around the world will increasingly require that each company possess IT competence and have access to professional networks and systems of communication.

On the other hand, we have shown that imaginary organizations existed long before modern information technology became a reality. IT is not the only possible cohesive force in an imaginary organization. Examples include important subsystems of IKEA, the classic system of advancing working capital in the textile industry of the past, and the venerable Hermods institute of correspondence. Certainly all of these arrangements were based on an innovative approach to distribution, contacts, and co-ordination, but advanced information technology was not necessary to implement the concept of the business.

As for companies established today, the situation may well be different. At least in our case studies on such companies, IT has played a major part from the very beginning in setting up customer data bases, co-ordinating far-flung systems of production, transferring knowledge within the imaginary organization, and keeping the business from coming apart.

CONSTRUCTION KIT

We can now summarize our reasoning on imaginary organizations and core competence and tie it in with the Figures in the first chapter.

In the emerging new imaginary organization, the IO-leader builds further on his own core competence with the help of an explicit or intuitive strategic map of what is needed to make the operation work. Adding partner enterprises, perhaps including partners who can provide delivery systems and various systems for co-ordination, is what we may refer to as *resourcing* (Figure 14.1). The imaginary new company is made up of a variety of co-ordinated resources.

Also in later phases of the life of a company, core competence is an actual and potential platform for strategies of growth. Such strategies may be implemented by conventional companies or in an imaginary organization.

A mature company may subsequently need to review its business and simplify, improve, and perhaps also sell off certain units. In such a situation the concept of *outsourcing* may be relevant. The analysis is the same, and here, too, the perspective of the IO is quite useful. The company reassesses its business, *starting with the market and proceeding backwards.* With an utterly critical eye, management analyses its concept of business (markets, services and products, systems of delivery, etc.) and then asks itself what units will be of vital importance in the future for making the business work. The analysis may indicate that certain functions no longer serve a useful purpose and should be sold or discontinued. Other functions, which might be performed better by someone else, become candidates for outsourcing. Still others might be improved and simplified, while remaining under the company's own roof.

There is an important difference both in theory and in practice between this approach and the many examples of company renovation in which the factory, production, or existing competence is taken as the starting point. With such a production-oriented perspective, it is easy to conclude that the market, not the company, is wrong. There are simply too few customers, and the remedy attempted, usually without success, is to stimulate the purchase of

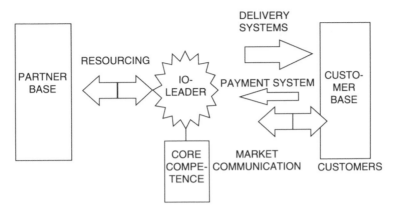

Figure 14.1 The imaginary organization

existing products by subsidizing them, and—treating the revenue lost as a "promotion expense" as it is called at some companies. But it is essential to understand the reality of today, and still more so of tomorrow, that *the resource in short supply is the customer*. It is then smarter to redimension the factory or, using an IO perspective, to pick your team according to the game you are going to play.

THE COMPANIES IN OUR CASES: OLD AND NEW, SERVICE INDUSTRIES AND ENGINEERING PRODUCTS

Some of the companies in our case studies may seem a little out of the ordinary. They deal in research, conferences, music, education, and high technology. But we have also shown that the IO perspective is applicable to SAS, IKEA, Hemglass, and parts of Alfa Laval. Engineering products are represented by Lorentzen·& Wettre and SATT Control. We are convinced that the number of more conventional examples of imaginary organizations will grow rapidly as more people begin to see the world in an IO perspective. This statement may be particularly true of the new industries which provide services and experiences rather than physical goods as such.

To summarize: an IO is an important part of several well known and successful companies. Imaginary organizations were built up and developed long before modern information technology entered the scene. However, modern IT radically increases the opportunities to create successful new IO structures. An IO perspective makes it easier to understand, and to criticize, the development strategies currently followed by a number of today's companies. Seeing the opportunities to build imaginary organizations will make it easier for management and business developers to concentrate operations and establish a basis for new strategies of development. For newly started companies with limited resources and ability to attract capital, the IO perspective may reveal a possible way to realize a concept of business in the face of adverse reality. The perspective may also make it easier for existing companies to respond quickly to new competition or to incorporate new technology.

CONSTITUENT ELEMENTS AND TYPICAL PROBLEM SITUATIONS

An imaginary organization, whether it takes the form of a new company or is set up and strengthened by developing an existing enterprise, is the result of an act of will. For the sake of simplicity, we attribute this will to an IO-leader. This individual, or group, is guided by a strategic vision and an IO perspective while attempting to build and develop an imaginary organization. The principal elements of the IO are:

- A customer base.
- A vision.
- A base of its own (core competence).
- A base of potential partners.
- A system for delivery.
- A system for co-ordinating production.
- Other communication systems for sharing knowledge.
- A system for payment.

The system is held together by different forces of attraction; the most important of these are a shared concept of business, often a boundary-transcending organizational culture, and a concept of personnel for all involvees.

Clear synergies and other "win–win" arrangements complete the picture. Certain kinds of collaboration may be governed by a contract, such as a royalty agreement or a profit-sharing system, whereas others—which may be quite important—are not at all regulated by legal instruments but are based on the candor, trust, and loyalty in a long-term business relationship.

Those *problems* which are described in our case studies, and for which an IO approach would appear to be effective, are related to:

- Building new companies and creating conditions for growth with limited resources (lack of equity capital, or tight budgetary constraints).

- Restoring or improving profitability in companies which have lost their focus and their edge.

- Quickly and forcefully responding to new competitive situations.

- Quickly and flexibly acquiring new competence or meeting the challenge of a new technology.

- Building bridges and establishing collaboration between different professional cultures.

- Strengthening a negotiating position or establishing a new position for achieving dominance on established markets.

These examples are taken from our case studies, and they are subject to the same limitations which we have previously mentioned concerning the companies described. There are surely a number of other, and perhaps more important, problem situations in which an IO perspective could prove fruitful.

ESSENTIAL RESOURCES—COMPETENCE, THE SPIRIT OF PERSONAL RESPONSIBILITY, AND THE SPIRIT OF TEACHING

A skillful leader enterprise deliberately cultivates the competence of the involvees and their companies. The opportunity to develop is an important element of the arrangement. In a simple market arrangement, which can be terminated on notice, both leader and partner enterprises will use their negotiating power to squeeze concessions out of each other. In an imaginary organization, all parties find that they gain from the relationship. Know-how is beneficial in itself; it enlarges the commercial pie to be shared. As time passes, involvees can do more and better business, both within and outside the IO. For this reason, they give up some of their short-term goals and ambitions. If this arrangement is to work, the IO-leader must be a very talented theatrical director, capable of circumventing the danger that one party may try to put pressure on the others, or that the involvees may feel used and withdraw from the arrangement.

Many, although far from all, of the companies in our case studies may be characterized as knowledge-intensive. Their principal resources are the people involved in the business, and/or the ideas, models, and systems which hold the operation together. Know-how and competence are more important than the supply of risk capital. In fact, an IO arrangement may have been chosen precisely because the IO-leader lacked capital in the conventional sense, or because it was difficult to provide security acceptable to external creditors, given the nature of the business.

Some sort of superior concept is implicit in the innovative character of the IO. The concept may relate to the market, to some new combination, to new methods of distribution, or even to the commercialization of a new system for payment. "I had this idea about distribution"—said Ingvar Kamprad, the founder and chairman of IKEA, in a conversation we recently had with him.

Person-to-person contact is easy in small, new, imaginary organizations. On a personal level, both the IO-leader and the involvees must devote considerable effort to finding the right incentives for all parties. In several of our case studies, we have seen how the IO-leader has shown great skill in this respect. Nevertheless, there are clear limits to the leverage attainable with such an approach. In spite of what we have said about declining costs of co-ordination because of information technology and other factors, the IO-leader cannot maintain an unlimited number of contacts.

The concept of work is based on the assumption that independence is of central importance to employees and other involvees in their jobs. It also implies that they want to know and understand what is happening in the business. Decisions by others are not accepted until they are understood and the alternatives have been presented. These people want to contribute their competence and do not like to be overlooked. It is important for them to know how their competence can be used and developed further. An active spirit of service is required of employees and other involvees; they must know their own capabilities and limits, while also assuming a responsibility for the development of others.

The function of the IO-leader is to set goals and to evaluate performance accordingly, but even more, it is to create conditions favorable to learning. Their role is to help employees and other involvees to learn from experience.

The focus of those who lead is thus neither leadership nor management, but a spirit of teaching—the emphasis is on helping employees and other involvees to acquire the capacity to learn from change, to promote innovation, and to manage and develop themselves.

IMAGINARY ORGANIZATIONS CREATE A NEED FOR NEW RESEARCH AND PRACTICE IN THE PROBLEMS RELATED TO TRANSCENDING BOUNDARIES

Imaginary organizations extend far beyond their formal boundaries, and thus also the frontiers of accepted practice and conventional systems of support in regard to accounting, leadership, valuation of companies, and legal responsibilities and rights. We have identified a number of new functions which must be developed before adequate leadership can be provided, and we have noted that several aspects of this enlarged concept of leadership are already being discussed by both personnel administrators and researchers on the subject of leadership.

We have also attempted to specify the needs for development in accounting and models for the valuation of an enterprise when the focus is not limited to a single company. Regrettably, our discussion must be rather hypothetical and speculative. To our knowledge, existing research in accounting offers little in the way of forward-looking encouragement. From this pessimistic observation, we may conclude that methods for company analysis, auditing, and provision of risk capital in regard to imaginary organizations remain to be developed.

Finally, it is clear that the legal foundation and certain rules of the game must be established as soon as possible. As long as imaginary organizations are successful and are used as systems for doing business in growth areas, these problems may not be so conspicuous. But when events turn for the worse, when losses must be sustained, product liability determined, or IO structures dissolved, these legal problems will be in the spotlight. Who owns assets which are unreported or difficult to value? How to divide up intangible property which is primarily the fruit of many years of joint development of competence, and which consists largely of jointly owned and well-established relationships with customers and suppliers?

Charles Handy (1994) comments on the need for legislation and a constructive set of rules to support the human organizations which in fact create value:

> The human association which in fact produces and distributes wealth, the association of workmen, managers, technicians and directors, is not an association recognised by the law. The association which the law does recognise—the association of shareholders, creditors and directors—is incapable of production and distribution and is not expected by the law to perform these functions. We have to give law to the real associations and to withdraw meaningless privilege from the imaginary one.

In our terminology, however, the need is precisely for laws and regulations to support "the imaginary one", although in substance we are in complete agreement with Handy. There are real organizations—dynamic, vigorous, and productive—in which we may find a superabundance of processes, but an absence of certain structures. And there are surely instances of companies in which the spirit of enterprise is dead and the life of the organization has withered away, a fact which no amount of formality and legislation can hide in the long run.

Imaginary organizations open up a new perspective. While no more real than other companies, they are real enough to deserve discovery by more people in a process which can lead to new enterprise, a vitalization of existing companies, and beneficial change in the structure of mature industries.

Take another look at the back cover illustration of this book. Discover the in-depth dimension of the picture. See how a new formation emerges. Then take a look at your company and/or your concept of business. Try to see how the imaginary organization takes shape in a new perspective-for action!

Appendix—Some Background Information on the Companies in our Case Studies

In this book we have shown how the management of each company in our case studies has dealt with a challenging situation. We will now provide some background information to give the reader a closer acquaintance and a better understanding of some of the companies. Our collection of case studies includes companies other than the ones described here and elsewhere in this book. At the same time, we are quite sure that many excellent examples of what we have been trying to demonstrate have thus far escaped our notice. Every time we speak about imaginary organizations at seminars and conferences, at least one listener comes forward to give us a tip on an interesting new case. This experience gives us good reason to hope that our readers, too, will find that our examples have helped them to see their own case studies in a new perspective on business.

Grammofon AB BIS

BIS operates in a very small industry: classical music on CD. But in that area BIS is world-renowned to an extent unmatched by most Swedish manufacturers of consumer goods.

BIS has existed for some 20 years; in the past year, it issued nearly 100 different new CDs. All of the previous 700 titles are kept in stock. The discs are exported to some 35 countries. The best seller has sold well over 100,000 copies, while only about 1000 copies of some of the other recordings have been sold after several years.

BIS now has eight employees. Partners do the rest of the work: CD production, composition and printing of text supplements, marketing, and local sales. The most important partners are of course the artists, whom BIS has often helped along in their careers.

The special profile which BIS has developed appears to be due entirely to the way in which it has managed all these contacts. Robert von Bahr, the founder, combines the talents of musician, administrator, and sound technician. He would surely have made a successful manager for some performer. Instead, he became an entrepreneur who built up a company world-famous in its field. His style is also characterized by a desire to remain faithful to certain musicians and works of music whose recordings he himself has wanted to produce and distribute; he has kept them in stock regardless of how well they have sold. He is also a perfectionist, for example, when it comes to the choice of recording location. While most buyers will not even notice the difference, his insistence on high fidelity is probably the reason why artists, distributors, and in the final analysis also buyers, have remained faithful to BIS.

The Swedish Folkopera

The Swedish Folkopera was started in 1976 as an independent theater group. The three founders are still in charge. Today it enjoys the status of city theater. It puts on some 200 performances a year in its own theater and on tours. In 1994 it made guest appearances in New York and Jerusalem. Around 500 people are involved in Folkopera's productions. Total annual receipts have been approximately SEK 30 million in recent years. But there are only seven permanent employees and three or four persons on one-year contracts. Other personnel are engaged on a project basis (for a particular production). On-stage performers are selected by audition; as for the musicians, there are section leaders, each of whom is charged with staffing his/her particular group of musicians.

The obvious comparison is with the Royal Opera, with nearly 700 employees but ticket receipts not much greater than those of the Swedish Folkopera. The Royal Opera, which is only 9% self-financing, is much more heavily dependent on subsidies; Folkopera is able to finance over half of its expenses. However, this comparison is not really fair. The Royal Opera has a diverse repertory and an official responsibility for the art of opera, while Folkopera is free to remain on the outskirts and pick and choose.

The Swedish Folkopera also has its entourage of sponsors and an active association of listeners; over the years, it has gained substantial support among politicians. Its ambition from the start has been to build up an enterprise. But to make existing resources suffice, it has constantly borrowed the competence of others and cultivated its network:

- Artists will do a part for one autumn, then work somewhere else. After a year or two, they will come back, better than before. That way they contribute to the development of the Swedish Folkopera.

- The association of listeners, ticket agents at places of work, sponsor companies, the School of Opera, and certain foreign theaters are all important. Without them, it would have been impossible to modernize the theater or to have guest performances.

Management includes artists with a sense of administration and business. The Managing Director has a degree in business but also performs parts in the productions put on by Folkopera. This combination is conducive to the mutual confidence of management and the artists and to an openness to the other party's point of view.

KalmarSalen (Kalmar Convention Hall & Convention Bureau)

The small city of Kalmar is located on the southeast coast of Sweden, opposite the island of Öland. KalmarSalen, which is housed in the old steam mill near the Öland ferry landing, was ready for inauguration in 1990. It was built as a multi-purpose facility for concerts and other public events, congresses, and conferences. The Managing Director of KalmarSalen, Marguerite Nilsson, was formerly Director of Marketing at Orrefors, a Swedish glassworks famous for its quality crystal. In her work, she is backed up by a foundation with strong support in business and other sectors of society.

KalmarSalen is the hub of a growing visitor and tourist industry in Kalmar. The components are:

- The concert hall.

- Hotel rooms in the city.
- The congress and conference business.
- Meals.
- Transportation.
- Participant administration.

In late 1993, the permanent core of the business consisted of four employees (equivalent to three full-time positions), including the Managing Director. In the fall of 1996, the number of employees had grown to 5 and the sales volume had increased by more than 50%. There is a parent company, Kongresshallen i Kalmar AB. Shares at SEK 25,000 apiece have been purchased by 104 companies and a number of private individuals.

KalmarSalen arranges and co-ordinates large and small congresses, conferences, and public events. All services are purchased from outside, except for central administration, marketing, and lobbying. Catering, reception, and cloakroom services are provided by Kalmar-sund Service, which belongs to the Samhall group, an employer of the handicapped. Under the terms of a general agreement, the services are specially requisitioned for each project. Events featuring performing artists are normally arranged by outside agents. KalmarSalen is rarely willing to assume the risk of holding a concert itself. Sound and lighting are furnished by Audio System, a small company with its own niche in that field. The auditorium, the artist, the concert surroundings, and the atmosphere of the intermissions all contribute to the total experience. Each party contributes, and bears the responsibility for, what its business has to offer.

Most of the business of KalmarSalen consists in arranging congresses and conferences. Marguerite Nilsson spends the bulk of her time attracting conferences. Her methods include direct personal contacts, direct marketing and traditional marketing and, above all, lobbying with professional groups who can steer their congress to Kalmar.

The few permanent employees of the leader enterprise offer the customer efficient administration of the project before, during, and after the conference. The following services are provided:

- Project management/consultation—project planning and budgeting, purchase of services, preparation of printed materials, press contacts, exhibition service, and (when required) financing.

- Participant administration—takes care of registration, accommodation, travel planning, etc.

- Budgeting and financial management—a complete financial department in miniature for the customer's project, the conference.

A number of these services are subsequently performed by co-operating consultants and small businesses. But the customer is always dealing one-on-one with KalmarSalen. From start to finish, one of KalmarSalen's project managers is in charge. In addition to the four individuals at the center of events, up to 150 people may be involved to assure that participants' meetings, food, leisure time, and rest are provided for.

Naturally, the imaginary organization of KalmarSalen can differ in size and competence depending on the arrangement. During 1993/94, arrangements included a Social Democratic youth conference (700 participants for one week), a meeting of the commission of the UNESCO council (50 delegates from the Nordic countries), a concentrated course for the Swedish Labor Market Board (film, multislide presentations, and theater), and a one-day conference for the Chamber of Commerce. In 1996 the size of the average arrangement had increased notably.

Towards the end of 1996 Marguerite Nilsson, the Managing Director, could look back at a very successful year, with increased internationalization and average growing size, and the profitibility of arrangements and events. Her small staff of women only has grown from 3.5 to 5. The staff consists of professionals for example a former auditor, an MBA, an IT expert, etc. The year ahead looks even more promising, since the city of Kalmar is going to celebrate its role as the capital of the "Kalmar Union" in 1397 which united the Nordic Countries in the early medieval age. Heads of state will assemble, and large conventions have been attracted to the facilities during the jubilee.

The staff take on more consultative roles towards partners and collaborators. A clear attempt is made to provide explicit value-added services to convention holders. The staff also assist in finding sponsors, planning spouses' programs, distributing information, etc. A www. homepage is underway and will be located at the web site of the City of Kalmar.

However, technology and IT still play modest roles. "We are building internal standard operating procedures", says Ms. Nilsson. "And we are above all building personal trust. It is individuals rather than organizations who constitute and develop our networks".

IMIT

IMIT, the Institute for Management of Innovation and Technology, was established in 1979. The founders were professors from the Swedish Institute of Management, Chalmers Institute of Technology, the Royal Institute of Technology, the Stockholm School of Economics, and the Lund Institute of Technology.

IMIT is a scholarly institution which initiates, supports, and organizes research and development in technological advancement and administration, and participates in education in these areas. Its objective is to "build bridges" between the two cultures which are the foundation of Swedish industry: the culture of technology and engineers, and that of business management and financial experts. IMIT's function is to contribute to the dissemination of knowledge through research projects, scholarly and popular reports, and continuing education of business-school graduates, engineers, researchers, and executives.

IMIT is charged with ensuring that interdisciplinary research is conducted through collaboration among the different founding institutions. A structure has been built up on the basis of six program areas, each with its own program manager.

IMIT provides a setting for efficient and productive research by:

- Organizing projects (i.e., marketing, arranging financing, staffing).
- Providing efficient project accounting and management.
- Organizing seminars.
- Organizing various forums for the exchange of ideas between researchers and practicians.
- Conducting information and PR activities.

IMIT has 11 employees. Professor Bengt Stymne is the Director, a half-time position. There are two full-time employees and four program managers, employed part-time. Administrative duties are shared by four people (a business manager, a project administrator, a person in charge of public-relations, and a secretary).

However, there are some 100 people on the payroll (the equivalent of 40–50 man-years). They are usually employed by one of the founding institutions. The ratio of involvees to employees is thus roughly 10:1. In addition, many other people, employees at various industrial companies, are involved as interviewees or members of reference groups and the like.

Total receipts in 1993 were approximately SEK 30 million, and economic performance satisfactory. Financially, projects vary in size from SEK 100,000 to 40 million, a typical project budget being around SEK 400,000.

IMIT's "customers" are companies and institutes of higher learning in need of developing their competence. IMIT's primary function is to pass on to them know-how in technology and leadership. The actual "service" provided by the system surrounding IMIT is thus research, studies, and a certain amount of continuing education. The principal resources required are the researchers in the network.

IMIT's contribution to the creation of value—and thus its core competence—lies in:

1. Matching important issues in industry with appropriate researchers.
2. Maintaining good relations with potential sources of financing.
3. Providing efficient project management through quality administration.

AB Svenska Pressbyrån

Pressbyrån is conveniently nearby and open for quick and convenient shopping by "people on the go". Good locations are sought at places where the traffic situation is favorable, and the assortment of products is adapted to the needs of passer-by customers. The key words in the concept of business are: chain of stores, easy to get to, basic product assortment, quality, employees, and the Pressbyrån profile.

Pressbyrån goes back a long way. The distribution of newspapers and magazines was started by Svenska Telegrambyrån in 1899 and taken over by the newly established Svenska Pressbyrån in 1906. For a long time the company was jointly owned by 130 Swedish newspapers, until it was acquired in 1991 by the Axel Johnson group; today it belongs to a subsidiary of that group, Axel Johnson Service HandelsGruppen AB (AX-S).

Half of the stores are owned by Pressbyrån, the other half by independent storekeepers with the same profile, product assortment, and marketing. Some 2200 people (equivalent to 1400 full-time positions) are employed in the part of the business wholly owned by Pressbyrån. Total sales of Pressbyrån in 1993 exceeded SEK 2 billion, of which wholly owned stores accounted for 1.3 billion and independently owned stores for 550 million. Pressbyrån has a market share of around 9% of the total convenience-store trade in Sweden. During the past 10 years, there has been a deliberate effort to transform the old news-stands into miniature department stores, under the Pressbyrån name. The store business accounted for about 85% of total sales. Every day some 350,000 people are served by Pressbyrån at its 430 locations all over Sweden. The product assortment includes newspapers and magazines, candy, soft drinks, and a variety of everyday commodities. Pressbyrån is also an agent for the various lotteries, off-track betting, and bus tickets. The Pressbyrån chain includes a number of cafeterias under the name of Regnbågen (transl: the Rainbow).

SCF

The mission of SCF (= Svenska Civilekonomföreningen; transl. the Swedish Association of School of Economics Graduates) is to further continuing professional education in management control and business administration, and to contribute to a healthy and comprehensive debate in these areas.

Since 1992, SCF has been a national organization for professionals in economics and business; thus, its membership is no longer restricted to people with the degree of "civilekonom", i.e. graduates of a Swedish school of economics and business administration.

The operations of SCF include:

• The program of continuing education, with intensive courses in the following areas: managerial economics/controllership, business management, special subjects such as the art of persuasion, and preparation for the CES diploma in management control. The total number of participant days (number of course days multiplied by the number of participants) is around 4000.

- Holding examinations for the CES diploma.
- Publication of six annual issues of the association's magazine, *Ekonomi & Styrning* (an appropriate English title might be "Financial and Management Control"), reported circulation 7400.
- Local associations and chapters.
- Member benefits, including the magazine mentioned above, discounts on subscriptions to various other magazines and newspapers, a set of insurance policies, and loans to members.

SCF has three permanent employees. They hold an imaginary organization together, in which approximately 250 people are involved, some 220 of them on a fairly permanent basis. SCF is active throughout the country.

Lorentzen & Wettre

Lorentzen & Wettre supplies the world's pulp and paper companies with advanced equipment for product control and process optimization. It enjoys a position as market leader and leader in quality.

The company is a subsidiary in the process-industry business area of the Cardo group. It is highly specialized, with a strategy of establishment in limited market segments, or niches. Approximately 90% of sales—SEK 235 million in 1996—are to foreign customers, through sales and service subsidiaries in the USA, Canada, Germany, Finland, France, and Norway, as well as affiliates in Singapore and Austria. In 25 other countries, sales and technical service are managed by distributors and agents. Research, product development, and assembly are located at the company's facilities in Stockholm. In 1995, there were 180 employees, 100 of them in Stockholm.

Lorentzen & Wettre is much more than a supplier of products. It could more appropriately be termed a know-how company. Its philosophy is to provide support to its customers. This commitment goes far beyond furnishing quality products and service; it extends to advanced research for developing solutions to deal with the measurement problems of customers, and to spread the results through training, books, articles, and lectures. Lorentzen & Wettre has a comprehensive training program to help customers to understand and make the best use of the company's products. As just indicated, research and product development not only results in new and modified products, but also in the production and dissemination of books, articles, and other writings. These are often cited in journals and elsewhere. Another way in which Lorentzen & Wettre functions as a know-how company is through close contact with institutes of research at colleges and universities. One consequence has been that a professor, expert in ultrasound, has been retained to participate in a development project.

The customer base consists of some 1000 pulp and paper mills. Around 40% of sales are made through subsidiaries, 30% through agents, and 30% directly from Sweden. Customers are very demanding and knowledgeable. Given the company's business of providing them with advanced measuring instruments, research and development is the leading function. Since these instruments are complex, and downtime in production at a mill is very costly, service is also a core area.

The core competence of the company is its leadership in know-how on equipment for product control and process optimization. The strategy for increasing sales is to make more customers realize that they can raise their profits by improving the quality of their paper products and the efficiency of their production process. Here the advanced measuring instruments provided by Lorentzen & Wettre fulfill an essential function.

The Värmdö Municipal Office of Cultural Affairs

Värmdö is a semirural community east of Stockholm. It is a separate "kommun", or municipality, with its own Office of Cultural Affairs (Värmdö kommuns kultursekretariat). The Office works through politicians, associations, and others who are in a position to further the overall policy objective that cultural activities should be a service demanded by all age groups and in all kinds of areas.

The core of the operation consists in the arrangements put on by the Office itself and in the advice and support which it furnishes to organizations involved in cultural activities, such as associations and educational federations. The Office also issues opinions on proposed plans and applications for building permits, for the purpose of safeguarding sites and buildings of historic value, and it provides information designed to bring to life the cultural heritage of the municipality.

The Office is staffed by a secretary of cultural affairs and two other employees. In addition, there are numerous involvees. These include contacts at associations and other organizations, school officials responsible for the arts, various councils and joint boards, and enthusiastic supporters. It has a budget of SEK 2.3 million.

By operating as it does, the Office can help associations to accomplish more with the subsidies they receive, and along lines consistent with the cultural ambitions of the municipality. A good example is the program of artistic activities at the schools. Here the Office attempts to involve the schools in exposing students to various forms of culture. At first the schools and their cultural officials were very cautious. Today they believe that they offer good programs and that the credit is theirs rather than that of the Office. This outcome was a deliberate result of the strategy adopted by the Office: to do most of the work while winning the support of the schools, and by helping them to create value while giving them a sense of participation and the credit for the success achieved.

The Office has also succeeded in persuading associations and educational federations active in similar areas to work together and to establish joint projects for mutual support and exchange of experience. In this way the parties involved can obtain more for their money, and the additional value created furthers the cultural ambitions of the municipality. Examples include a local historic preservation council and a council for the cultural environment. Contacts and co-operation have been favored by an exchange of annual reports. Also, a degree of formal control is exercised by the Office through subsidy guidelines which it has prepared and follows in practice. In the voluntary councils (such as the local historic preservation council), statements of common objectives are drafted and later reviewed in joint meetings, through visits, and by some exchange of statistics.

The Office of Cultural Affairs offers an opportunity for the various parts of its network of contacts to create new value. It makes available an extensive store of knowledge, a network in the municipality which includes all the different associations involved in cultural activities, the local politicians, and the various parties with a commercial interest in cultural activities.

The Office exercises different kinds of leadership in different parts of the network of contacts. It has learned to work through others and without regard to its own prestige.

The Stockholm Stock Exchange

The mission of the Stockholm Stock Exchange (Stockholms Fondbörs) is to meet the need for provision of capital, determination of market value, and investment opportunities by offering the services of a marketplace for trading in securities to members, issuers of stock, and investors.

The classic image of the stock market—the floor of the Exchange swarming with brokerage-firm employees running, shouting, and telephoning—has been put away in the photo album. Today the same business is done by means of highly efficient, modern information systems, computerized telephone exchanges, and coded telecommunications.

In order for the Exchange to be "the best marketplace for trading in Swedish securities", there must be a strong infrastructure of IT systems which can "provide low-cost information and facilitate searching", to permit reliable and cost-effective "matching of orders to buy and sell financial instruments, and completion of the resulting transactions".

The stock exchange which its President, Bengt Rydén, directs today bears little resemblance to the one which existed when he assumed his position some 10 years ago. Trading is normally done through intermediaries—stockbrokers—who are members of the Exchange. The Stockholm Stock Exchange is a Swedish corporation (aktiebolag). The Swedish Stock Exchange Act (Börslagen) states that "the Exchange shall only be open to members". But times are changing. The concept of membership and the Swedish Stock Corporation Act (ABL = Aktiebolagslagen) belong to another world.

The Stockholm Stock Exchange Corporation (Stockholms Fondbörs AB) has 60 employees, of whom 25 are charged with maintenance and development of computerized systems and administrative procedures. Another 15 monitor trade and compile statistics. Seven or eight are involved in accounting and administration, and a few in market information. A total of five people make up management and fill certain specialist positions. In the opinion of the President, the total number of employees should be kept constant even though continued strong growth is expected in production and sales.

In 1987 the decision was made "to go electronic". Trading was to be based on a technically new system known as SAX. Certain functions have been added to permit the Exchange to offer other services such as trading in bonds (SOX) and money-market instruments (SMX).

The Stockholm Stock Exchange Corporation is surrounded by four clusters of stakeholders: members who operate through the Exchange, owners who now are stockholders of the Exchange, issuers of securities who use the Exchange to raise capital, and suppliers of services which range from food (a restaurant run by a catering service) to development and maintenance of the systems of exchange. To a limited extent, the Exchange rents facilities, and is itself a major host or organizer of seminars, on its own or for others, related to the activities of stock exchanges, the national economy, or company analyses.

A member council, a corporate council, and an investor council act as reference groups and provide a forum for exchange of information between Exchange management and major stakeholder groups.

That the Exchange operates as an imaginary organization has become quite apparent in recent years after floor trading was stopped. Trading then spread throughout the country and even abroad. Thus, in a number of cases the Exchange has been brought closer to customers. It has also become more abstract and depersonalized. The fellowship of brokers has had to give way to a network community. Gone is the sweat of people running across the floor, and body language and facial expressions can no longer influence market quotations.

The basic nature of the Exchange as a market and meeting place for innumerable independent actors remains unaltered, but eye contact and meeting face-to-face have been replaced by ear contact and meeting over a network, thus accentuating the abstract and imaginary character of the system of stock trading.

CE Fritzes

CE Fritzes is a publishing enterprise which specializes in issuing information on legal norms set by the national government (laws and regulations); recipients are persons who use this information for decision-making in a professional capacity. The purpose is to make it easier for customers to practice their professions in a progressive and correct manner, and thus to make better decisions. CE Fritzes would like to be regarded as a professional, flexible, and friendly company which treats every customer as a unique individual.

The corporation CE Fritzes AB was formed in 1991. As of 1994, it had five principal units (Aktuell Juridik, Allmänna Förlaget, Norstedts Juridik, Publica, and Fritzes InformationsCenter). The company of today is the product of a series of mergers. Its origins can be traced to 1834, when the Norstedts press began to print *Svensk Författningssamling* (the Swedish Code of Statutes) and to publish legal literature. In 1837 Carl Eduard Fritze started a book store in Stockholm. Well over a century later, in 1969, we come to the next milestone: the establishment of Allmänna Förlaget (AF, the Government Publishing House) as a separate corporation under the Department of Finance; AF was charged with co-ordinating production and distribution of government printing. In 1970 operations were transferred to Liber Grafiska AB. In January, 1991, the Liber group was in turn acquired by Wolter Kluwer, a Dutch publisher.

In 1993, sales exceeded SEK 200 million, and there were 1109 employees. The company's operations are located in Sweden.

Normative information of quality has long been communicated on paper in the form of books and documents, and outside Sweden under systems of subscription to loose-leaf materials. The CD-ROM technology was developed in the 1980s as a new way to transmit information. Management was aware of the potential of the new technology and its future strategic importance. They also realized that the company lacked competence in the area. In 1991 they were facing the choice of either first starting their own in-house program to develop the necessary competence in CD-ROM before attempting to commercialize the new technology, or proceeding directly to commercial development while obtaining the necessary competence from outside.

Management chose the latter course, mainly because it would take less time. Commercial introduction at an early date was considered important. The required competence would be built up during the course of the project as the outside specialists involved in it passed on their know-how to the company.

For a publishing enterprise to choose an IO solution would appear normal. It would be no wild guess to assume that running a company primarily engaged in publishing would be precisely a question of "management in imaginary organizations". But not at all in this case. On the contrary, CE Fritzes—like most publishers—assumes a passive, even subservient posture toward writers. Government materials are published through Allmänna Förlaget largely on the terms set by the issuing authority. In the case of Norstedts Juridik (Norstedts Legal Publications), the author submits the manuscript for printing, binding, and distribution to readers. The editor meekly asks, "When might Professor X expect to be submitting his comments on this statute?" The editor would never dare to make revisions or to comment on the content. The book will be published when the professor is ready.

Scandinavian PC Systems

SPCS, Scandinavian PC Systems, was founded in the mid-1980s. In some 10 years, sales have risen from SEK 1 million to SEK 100 million, with fair to good profitability despite the rapid growth of the company. Starting with the two founders, the number of employees increased to about 50; thereafter, it was reduced to around 25, while the rate of growth was maintained. A conventional company analysis by an outsider would produce a slightly confusing, and in some ways very impressive, set of key ratios. Most bankers and even venture capitalists would still remain unsure about putting a value on the company. For SPCS is different.

SPCS produces, supplies, and sells PC programs for IBM-compatible computers in Windows and DOS environments. The essential strategy has been to develop simple, easy-to-use basic programs for sale at astonishingly low prices (often only one-eighth or one-tenth that of the market leader). The programs are sold largely by mail order, and in high volumes. During the company's brief existence, it has become the market leader in terms of volume in its product areas. The first programs were for word-processing, calculation, and registers. Then programs for bookkeeping, taxes, and payroll were added. Today there are also more advanced programs for management control, CAD/CAM, desktop publishing, and systems for experts.

Right from the start, SPCS was organized differently than its competitors. Companies that sell programs are supposed to employ programmers. However, SPCS regarded itself more as a kind of publisher, with the producers, like writers, receiving royalties. SPCS controlled various networks of suppliers and, above all, customer contacts. At trade fairs, and through advertising and its own high-quality bimonthly customer magazine with a circulation of around 100,000 copies, the company has developed and maintains a very interesting arrangement for customer communication. As with its neighbor in southern Sweden, IKEA, the annual catalog is an absolutely central vehicle for sales promotion. The customer data base, and the register of involvees who are not employees, are perhaps the principal assets of SPCS.

SPCS is the spider in a web of operations, co-ordinating product development as well as production, marketing, and distribution. The PC programs are created by external individual experts or, increasingly often, by co-operating companies. The customer magazine is produced by an outside enterprise. The Scandinavian PC Training program is conducted by a partly owned subsidiary. Distribution is a separate business which is not owned by SPCS. The company is even considering the sale of the customer service unit to the employees.

Over the years, the founders of SPCS have proven very adept at letting the company grow without becoming large and cumbersome. They have sold most but not all of their ownership interest to the Swedish Savings Banks, while retaining the initiative in the development of the business. In recent years SPCS has entered into new alliances, such as the one with Computer Associates, CA, a large American company. Later they bought back ownership control and brought in new financial partners as owners. In the Spring of 1997, SPCS was introduced on the Swedish OTC Stock Exchange.

The customers of SPCS range from price-conscious individuals (who pay out of their own pockets), to managers appreciative of the simplicity of the programs, to customers who are so enterprising and knowledgeable that they gradually become "pro-sumers", customers who contribute actively to product development.

High-quality instruction manuals (with a hard cover and with program discs placed under the front cover of the manual, which is enclosed in a plastic coating) complete the picture. The books are so well written and detailed that the customer normally can use the program on his/her own without requiring a costly level of customer service.

References

Arbnor, I., Borglund, S-E. & Liljedahl, T. (1980). *Osynligt ockuperad; En arkeologisk studie av nutidens ledarskap*. Liber Läromedel, Malmö.

Arbnor, I. et al (1993). *Affärskvalitet som livsidé*. Förlagshus Öster om Leden AB, Brösarp.

Argyris, C. & Schön, D.A. (1978). *Organizational Learning*. Addison-Wesley, Reading, MA.

Bartlett, C.A. & Ghoshal, S. (1994). Changing the role of top management: beyond strategy to purpose. *Harvard Business Review*, Nov–Dec.

Box, G.E.P & Draper, N.R, (1969). *Evolutionary Operation*. Wiley, New York.

Campbell, D.T. (1969). Reforms as experiments. *American Psychologist*, **24**, 409–429.

Carlzon, Jan. (1987) *Moments of Truth*. Ballinger Publishing Co., Cambridge, Mass.

Chi, T. (1994). Trading in strategic resources: necessary conditions, transaction cost problems, and choice of exchange structure. *Strategic Management Journal*, **15**, (4), 271–290.

Coase, R. (1937). The Nature of the Firm. *Economica*, **4**, 386–405.

Davidow, W.H. & Malone, M.S. (1992). *The Virtual Corporation*. Harper Collins, New York.

de Meyer, A. (1993). *Managing the Post-lean Factory. Will it be the Virtual Factory?* INSEAD Paper.

Flamholtz, E. (1985). *Human Resource Accounting*. Jossey-Bass, San Francisco, CA.

Forrester, Jay. C. (1961). *Industrial Dynamics*. Wiley, New York.

Goold, M., Campbell, A. & Alexander, M. (1994). *Corporate-level Strategy. Creating Value in the Multibusiness Company*. Wiley, New York.

Greenleaf, R.K. (1977). *Servant Leadership*. Paulist Press, New York.

Grönroos (1990) *Service Management*. ISL Förlag, Göteborg.

Gummesson, E. (1995). Relationsmarknadsfö: Från 4P till 30R. Liber-Hermods, Malmö.

Gummesson, E. (1996) Relationship marketing and imaginary organizations. A synthesis. *European Journal of Marketing*, **30**(2), 31–44.

Hartman, R.S. (1967). *The Structure of Value: Foundations of a Scientific Axiology* Southern Illinois Press, Carbondale I.L.

Hamel, G. & Prahalad, C.K. (1994). *Competing for the Future.* Harvard Business School Press. Cambridge, MA.

Hamel, G. & Heene A. (eds) (1994). *Competence-based Competition.* Wiley, Chichester.

Hammarkvist, K.O, Håkansson, H. & Mattsson, L.-G. (1982). *Marknadsföring för konkurrenskraft.* Almkvist & Wiksell, Stockholm.

Handy, C. (1989). *The Age of Unreason.* Business Books, London.

Handy, C. (1994). *The Empty Raincoat.* Hutchinson, London.

Hedberg, B.L.T, Nystrom, P.C. & Starbuck, W.H. (1976) Camping on seesaws: prescriptions for a self-designing organization. *Administrative Science Quarterly,* **21,** 41-65.

Hedberg, B.L.T. & Jönsson, S.A. (1978). Designing semi-confusing information systems for organizations in changing environments. *Accounting, Organizations, and Society,* **3,** 47-64.

Hirschmann, A.O. (1970). *Exit, Voice, and Loyalty; Responses to Decline in Firms, Organizations, and States.* Harvard University Press, Cambridge, MA.

Hägg, I. & Johansson, J. (eds) (1982), *Företag i nätverk-ny syn på konkurrenskraft* (Companies in Networks—A New View on Competitiveness). Studieförbundet Näringsliv och Samhälle, Stockholm.

INSEAD (1993). *Creating the Virtual Factory.* INSEAD Report, WP No. 9282.

Johannisson, B. (1992). *Entrepreneurs as learners—Beyond Education and Training.* Working Paper Series 1992/7, Institutet för ekonomisk forskning, Lund.

Johansson, U. & Nilsson, M. (1992). *Personalekonomiska beräkningar och besluts-fattande.* Personalekonomiska Institutets skriftserie No. 90:2, Stockholm.

Kaplan, R.S. & Norton, D.P. (1996). Using the balanced scorecard as a strategic management system. *Harvard Business Review,* Jan-Feb, 75-85.

Ljung, A., (1992). *Intressentstrategier.* EFI, Stockholm.

Martin, J.G. (1996). *The Great Transition.* AMACOM, New York.

Mintzberg, H. (1983). *Structures in Fives: Designing Effective Organization.* Prentice-Hall, Englewood Cliffs, NJ.

Mintzberg, H. (1989). *Mintzberg on Management.* Free Press, New York.

Morgan, G. (1993). *Imaginization. The Art of Creative Management.* Sage, Newbury Park, CA.

Moss Kanter, R. (1994). Collaborative advantage: the art of alliances. *Harvard Business Review,* July-August.

Normann, R. (1984). *Service Management.* Wiley, Chichester.

Norman, R. & Ramirez, R. (1993). From value chain to value constellation: designing interactive strategy. *Harvard Business Review,* **72,** July-Aug, 65-77.

Nystrom, P.C., Hedberg, B.L.T. & Starbuck, W.H. (1976). Interacting processes as organization designs. In Kilmann, R.H., Pondy, L.R. & Slevin, D.P. (eds), *The Management of Organization Design,* Vol. I, pp. 209-230. Elsevier, New York.

Peters, T. (1984). Strategy follows structure: developing distinctive skills. *California Management Review,* Spring.

Porter, M. (1985). *Competitive Advantage.* Free Press, New York.

Prahalad, C.K. & Hamel, G. (1990). The core competence of the corporation. *Harvard Business Review,* May-June.

Prahalad, C.K. (1993). A strategy for growth: the role of core competencies in the corporation. *EFMD Forum,* **93** (3-4), 3-10.

Quinn, J.B. (1992). *Intelligent Enterprise.* Free Press, New York.

Skandia (1996). *Value-creating Processes.* Supplement to Skandia's 1995 Annual Report.

Stalk, G., Evans, P. & Shulman, L. E. (1992). Competing on capabilities: the new rules of corporate strategy. *Harvard Business Review*, March-April.

Stewart, G.B. (1991). *The Quest for Value.* Harper, London.

Sveiby, K-E. & Risling, A. (1986). *Kunskapsföretaget.* Liber, Malmö.

Teece, D.J. (1992). Strategies for capturing the financial benefits from technological innovation. In Rosenberg, Nathan et al (eds), *Technology and the Wealth of Nations.* Stanford University Press, Stanford, CT.

Watzlawick, P., Weakland, J.H., & Fisch R. (1974). *Change.* Norton, New York.

Weick, K. (1979). Educational organizations as loosely coupled systems. *Administrative Science Quarterly*, **21**, 1-19.

Weick, K. (1995). *Sensemaking in Organizations.* Sage, Seven Oaks.

Welles, E.O. (1993). Virtual realities. *INC.*, August, 58-60.

Wikström, S. and Normann, R. et al (1994) *Knowledge and Values: A New Perspective on Corporate Transformation.* Routledge, London.

Williamson, O.E. (1975). *Markets and Hierarchies: Analysis and Antitrust Implications.* Vols. I & II. Free Press, New York.

Williamson, O.E. (1981). The economics of organization: the transaction cost approach. *American Journal of Sociology*, **87**(3) 548-577.

Index